D0091945

ROMANS

Grace, Truth, and Redemption

JOHN MACARTHUR

THOMAS NELSON
Since 1798

ROMANS
MACARTHUR BIBLE STUDIES

© 2007, John F. MacArthur, Jr.

All rights reserved. No portion of this book may be reproduced, stored in a retrieval system, or transmitted in any form or by any means—electronic, mechanical, photocopy, recording, scanning, or other—except for brief quotations in critical reviews or articles, without the prior written permission of the publisher.

John MacArthur
"Unleashing God's Truth, One Verse at at a Time®"
"Unleashing God's Truth, One Verse at a Time" is a trademark of Grace to You. All rights reserved.

Published in Nashville, Tennessee, by Nelson Books, an imprint of Thomas Nelson. Nelson Books and Thomas Nelson are registered trademarks of HarperCollins Christian Publishing, Inc.

Nelson Books titles may be purchased in bulk for education, business, fundraising, or sales promotional use. For information, please email SpecialMarkets@ThomasNelson.com

Published in association with the literary agency of Wolgemuth & Associates, Inc.

Produced with the assistance of the Livingstone Corporation. Project staff include Jake Barton, Betsy Todt Schmitt, and Andy Culbertson.

Project editors: Mary Horner Collins, Amber Rae, and Len Woods

Scripture quotations marked NKJV are taken from the The New King James Version®. © ww1982 by Thomas Nelson, Inc. Used by permission. All rights reserved.

"Keys to the Text" material taken from the following sources:

Galatians. MacArthur New Testament Commentary Series. © 1987, 1996 by John MacArthur. Published by Moody Press, Chicago, Illinois. Used by permission.

The Gospel According to Jesus. © 1997, 1988 by John MacArthur. (Electronic ed.). Published by Zondervan, Grand Rapids, Michigan. Used by permission.

The MacArthur Study Bible (electronic ed.), John MacArthur, General Editor. © 1997 by Word Publishing. All rights reserved. Used by permission.

Nelson's New Illustrated Bible Dictionary, Rev. ed. R. F. Youngblood, F. F. Bruce, R. K. Harrison, editors. © 1995 by Thomas Nelson Publishers. Used by permission.

Romans. MacArthur New Testament Commentary Series. © 1994, 1996 by John MacArthur. Published by Moody Press, Chicago, Illinois. Used by permission.

Cover Art by Holly Sharp Design
Interior Design and Composition by Joel Bartlett, Livingstone Corporation

ISBN 978-0-7180-3506-8

Printed in the United States of America.

HB 09.12.2022

Contents

Introduction to Romans 1

1 The Good News 5
Romans 1:1–17

2 The Bad News 13
Romans 1:18–3:20

3 By Faith Alone 23
Romans 3:21–4:25

4 Grace through One Man 33
Romans 5:1–21

5 Dead and Alive! 41
Romans 6:1–23

6 Delivered from the Law 49
Romans 7:1–25

7 In the Spirit 57
Romans 8:1–39

8 Israel and God's Eternal Plan 65
Romans 9:1–11:36

9 Supernatural Living 77
Romans 12:1–21

10 Living in the World 85
Romans 13:1–14

11 The Strong and the Weak 93
Romans 14:1–15:13

12 Ministering Together 103
Romans 15:14–16:27

Introduction to Romans

This epistle's name comes from its original recipients: the members of the church in Rome, the capital of the Roman Empire.

Author and Date

No one disputes that the apostle Paul wrote Romans. Like his namesake, Israel's first king (*Saul* was Paul's Hebrew name; *Paul* his Greek name), Paul was from the tribe of Benjamin (Phil. 3:5). He was also a Roman citizen (Acts 16:37; 22:25). Paul was born about the time of Christ's birth, in Tarsus, an important city (Acts 9:11; 21:39) in the Roman province of Cilicia located in Asia Minor (modern Turkey). He spent much of his early life in Jerusalem as a student of the celebrated rabbi Gamaliel (Acts 22:3). Like his father before him, Paul was a Pharisee (Acts 23:6), a member of the strictest Jewish sect (Phil. 3:5).

Miraculously converted while on his way to Damascus (ca. AD 33–34) to arrest Christians in that city, Paul immediately began proclaiming the gospel message (Acts 9:20). After narrowly escaping from Damascus with his life (Acts 9:23–25; 2 Cor. 11:32–33), Paul spent three years in Nabatean Arabia, south and east of the Dead Sea (Gal. 1:17–18). During that time, he received much of his doctrine as direct revelation from the Lord (Gal. 1:11–12).

More than any other individual, Paul was responsible for the spread of Christianity throughout the Roman Empire. He made three missionary journeys through much of the Mediterranean world, tirelessly preaching the gospel that he had once sought to destroy (Acts 26:9). After Paul returned to Jerusalem bearing an offering for the needy in the church there, he was falsely accused by some Jews (Acts 21:27–29), savagely beaten by an angry mob (Acts 21:30–31), and arrested by the Romans. Although two Roman governors, Felix and Festus, as well as Herod Agrippa, did not find him guilty of any crime, pressure from the Jewish leaders kept Paul in Roman custody. After two years, the apostle exercised his right as a Roman citizen and appealed his case to Caesar. Through a harrowing trip (Acts 27–28), including a violent, two-week storm at sea that culminated in a shipwreck, Paul reached Rome. Eventually Paul was released for a brief period of ministry, but he was later arrested again. Paul suffered martyrdom at Rome in ca. AD 65–67 (2 Tim. 4:6).

Though physically unimpressive (2 Cor. 10:10; Gal. 4:14), Paul possessed an inner strength granted him through the Holy Spirit's power (Phil. 4:13). The grace of God proved sufficient to provide for his every need (2 Cor. 12:9–10), enabling this noble servant of Christ to successfully finish his spiritual race (2 Tim. 4:7).

Paul wrote Romans from Corinth, as indicated by the references to Phoebe (Rom. 16:1, Cenchrea was Corinth's port), Gaius (Rom. 16:23), and Erastus (Rom. 16:23)—all of whom were associated with Corinth. The apostle wrote the letter toward the close of his third missionary journey (most likely in AD 56), as he prepared to leave for Palestine with an offering for the poor believers in the Jerusalem church (Rom. 15:25). Phoebe was given the great responsibility of delivering this letter to the Roman believers (16:1–2).

Background and Setting

Rome was the capital and most important city of the Roman Empire. It was founded in 753 BC, but is not mentioned in Scripture until New Testament times. Rome is located along the banks of the Tiber River, about fifteen miles from the Mediterranean Sea. Until an artificial harbor was built at nearby Ostia, Rome's main harbor was Puteoli, some hundred and fifty miles away. In Paul's day, the city had a population of over one million people, many of whom were slaves. Rome boasted magnificent buildings, such as the Emperor's palace, the Circus Maximus, and the Forum, but its beauty was marred by the slums in which so many lived. According to tradition, Paul was martyred outside Rome on the Ostian Way during Nero's reign (AD 54–68).

Some of those converted on the Day of Pentecost probably founded the church at Rome (Acts 2:10). Paul longed to visit the Roman church, but had been prevented from doing so (1:13). In God's providence, Paul's inability to visit Rome gave the world this inspired masterpiece of gospel doctrine.

Paul's primary purpose in writing Romans was to teach the great truths of the gospel of grace to believers who had never received apostolic instruction. The letter also introduced him to a church where he was personally unknown but hoped to visit soon for several important reasons: to edify the believers (1:11), to preach the gospel (1:15), and to get to know the Roman Christians so they could encourage him (1:12; 15:32), better pray for him (15:30), and help him with his planned ministry in Spain (15:28).

Unlike Paul's other epistles (for example, 1 Corinthians, 2 Corinthians, and Galatians), his purpose for writing Romans was not to correct aberrant theology or rebuke ungodly living. The Roman church was doctrinally sound, but, like all churches, it was in need of the rich doctrinal and practical instruction this letter provides.

Historical and Theological Themes

Since Romans is primarily a work of doctrine, it contains little historical material. Paul does use such familiar Old Testament figures as Abraham (chapter 4), David (4:6–8), Adam (5:12–21), Sarah (9:9), Rebekah (9:10), Jacob and Esau (9:10–13), and Pharaoh (9:17) as illustrations. He also recounts some of Israel's history (chapters 9–11). Chapter 16 provides insightful glimpses into the nature and character of the first-century church and its members.

The overarching theme of Romans is the righteousness that comes from God: the glorious truth that God justifies guilty, condemned sinners by grace alone through faith in Christ alone. Chapters 1–11 present the theological truths of that doctrine, while chapters 12–16 detail its practical outworking in the lives of individual believers and the life of the whole church. Some specific theological topics include principles of spiritual leadership (1:8–15); God's wrath against sinful humankind (1:18–32); principles of divine judgment (2:1–16); the universality of sin (3:9–20); an exposition and defense of justification by faith alone (3:21–4:25); the security of salvation (5:1–11); the transference of Adam's sin (5:12–21); sanctification (chapters 6–8); sovereign election (chapter 9); God's plan for Israel (chapter 11); spiritual gifts and practical godliness (chapter 12); the believer's responsibility to human government (chapter 13); and principles of Christian liberty (14:1–15:12).

Interpretive Challenges

As the preeminent doctrinal work in the New Testament, Romans naturally contains a number of difficult passages. Paul's discussion of the perpetuation of Adam's sin (5:12–21) is one of the deepest, most profound theological passages in all of Scripture. The nature of humanity's union with Adam and how Adam's sin was transferred to the human race has always been the subject of intense debate. Bible students also disagree on whether 7:7–25 describes Paul's experience as a believer or unbeliever or is a literary device and not intended to be autobiographical at all. The closely related doctrines of election (8:28–30) and the sovereignty of God (9:6–29) have confused many believers. Others question whether chapters 9–11 teach that God has a future plan for the nation of Israel. Some have ignored Paul's teaching on the believer's obedience to human government (13:1–7) in the name of Christian activism, while others have used it to defend slavish obedience to totalitarian regimes. Some of these interpretive challenges are addressed in the lessons that follow.

Notes

1

The Good News

Romans 1:1–17

Drawing Near

When and where did you first hear the gospel—the good news that Jesus loves you and died for your sins?

_____

_____

_____

What is so "good" about this good news of the gospel?

_____

_____

_____

As you begin this study, what do want to learn about the book of Romans? How do you want to grow in your faith?

_____

_____

_____

The Context

Newspapers and television news shows contain constant reminders that most news is bad and seems to be getting worse. What happens on a national and worldwide scale, however, is simply the magnification of what is occurring on an individual level. As personal problems, animosities, and fears increase, so do their counterparts in society at large. A terrifying power grips human beings at the very core of their being. Left unchecked, it pushes them to self-destruction in one form or another. That power is *sin*, and that is always bad news. The tidbits of good news are often merely brief respites from the bad. And sometimes what appears to be good merely masks an evil. One cynic commented that peace treaties merely provide time for both sides to reload.

The essence of Paul's letter to the Romans, however, is that there is good news that is truly good! The apostle was, in fact, "a minister of Jesus Christ to the Gentiles, ministering the gospel of God" (Rom. 15:16). He brought the good news that, in Christ, sin can be forgiven, selfishness can be overcome, guilt can be removed, anxiety can be alleviated, and people can, indeed, have hope and eternal glory.

The entire thrust of the book of Romans is distilled in the first seven verses. The apostle apparently was so overjoyed by his message of good news that he could not wait to introduce his readers to the gist of what he had to say. He burst into it immediately.

Keys to the Text

Apostle: "One who is sent with a commission." An apostle chosen and trained by Jesus Christ to proclaim His truth during the formative years of the church. In its primary usage, the term applied to the original twelve disciples who were chosen at the beginning of Jesus' earthly ministry, and were set aside to lay the foundation of the early church. They were also given power to perform healings and to cast out demons as verifying signs of their divine authority. Because Paul was not among the original twelve, he needed to defend his apostleship. One of the qualifications was witnessing the risen Christ (Acts 1:22). Paul explained to the Corinthian church that between His resurrection and ascension Jesus "was seen by Cephas [Peter], then by the twelve. . . . After that He was seen by James, then by all the apostles. Then last of all He was seen by me also" (1 Cor. 15: 5–8 NKJV). Paul witnessed the resurrected Christ in a unique way as he was traveling to Damascus to arrest Christians there (Acts 9). Further personal appearances of the Lord to Paul are recorded in Acts 18:9; 22:17–21; 23:11; and 2 Corinthians 12:1–4.

In a wider sense, the term *apostle* is also used of men like Barnabas, Silas, and Timothy (Rom. 16:7). Such men are more specifically called messengers (*apostoloi*) of the churches, whereas the Twelve and Paul were "apostles of Jesus Christ." Neither group was perpetuated. Except for Judas (who was replaced by Matthias), there is no record of an apostle in either the primary or secondary group being replaced after he died.

Unleashing the Text

Read 1:1–17, noting the key words and definitions next to the passage.

Romans 1:1–17 (NKJV)

1 *Paul, a bondservant of Jesus Christ, called to be an apostle, separated to the gospel of God*
2 *which He promised before through His prophets in the Holy Scriptures,*
3 *concerning His Son Jesus Christ our Lord, who was born of the seed of David according to the flesh,*
4 *and declared to be the Son of God with power according to the Spirit of holiness, by the resurrection from the dead.*
5 *Through Him we have received grace and apostleship for obedience to the faith among all nations for His name,*
6 *among whom you also are the called of Jesus Christ;*
7 *To all who are in Rome, beloved of God, called to be saints: Grace to you and peace from God our Father and the Lord Jesus Christ.*
8 *First, I thank my God through Jesus Christ for you all, that your faith is spoken of throughout the whole world.*
9 *For God is my witness, whom I serve with my spirit in the gospel of His Son, that without ceasing I make mention of you always in my prayers,*
10 *making request if, by some means, now at last I may find a way in the will of God to come to you.*
11 *For I long to see you, that I may impart to you some spiritual gift, so that you may be established—*
12 *that is, that I may be encouraged together with you by the mutual faith both of you and me.*
13 *Now I do not want you to be unaware, brethren, that I often planned to come to you (but was hindered until now), that I might have some fruit among you also, just as among the other Gentiles.*
14 *I am a debtor both to Greeks and to barbarians, both to wise and to unwise.*
15 *So, as much as is in me, I am ready to preach the gospel to you who are in Rome also.*

bondservant (v. 1)—the Greek word for servant or slave, but given a Hebrew sense here by Paul to imply willing service for a beloved, respected master

separated to (v. 1)—Paul had been set apart (that is, specially selected) by God for his ministry to the Gentiles.

gospel of God (v. 1)—The word *gospel* means "good news."

declared (v. 4)—Literally, "to distinguish, or mark off," this is the Greek word from which the English word "horizon" comes; as the horizon marks clearly the boundary between earth and sky, the resurrection marks Christ as the Son of God come in the flesh.

obedience to the faith (v. 5)—True saving faith always produces obedience and submission to the Lordship of Christ.

serve with my spirit (v. 9)—The word translated "serve" can also be translated "worship."

spiritual gift (v. 11)—The Greek word for "gift" is *charisma,* meaning a "gift of grace," a divine enablement.

debtor (v. 14)—under obligation to fulfill his ministry because of God's calling and the Gentiles' great need

salvation (v. 16)—deliverance or rescue, in this case from lostness—that is, separation from God

believes (v. 16)—trusts, relies on, or has faith in

16 *For I am not ashamed of the gospel of Christ, for it is the power of God to salvation for everyone who believes, for the Jew first and also for the Greek.*
17 *For in it the righteousness of God is revealed from faith to faith; as it is written, "The just shall live by faith."*

1) What does this passage reveal about the promise of the good news (v. 2) and the Person of the good news (vv. 3–4)?

2) Verses 8–15 provide interesting insights into Paul's character and motives, as well as the kind of behavior that should mark all true spiritual leaders. What admirable qualities are described in these verses?

(Verses to consider: 1 Thess. 2:1–3:13)

3) What reasons does Paul give for not being ashamed of the gospel?

Going Deeper

Read about Paul's own experience with the gospel and his commissioning by Christ to go to the Gentiles. This testimony is from Acts 26.

Acts 26:1–18 (NKJV)

1 *Then Agrippa said to Paul, "You are permitted to speak for yourself." So Paul stretched out his hand and answered for himself:*
2 *"I think myself happy, King Agrippa, because today I shall answer for myself before you concerning all the things of which I am accused by the Jews,*
3 *especially because you are expert in all customs and questions which have to do with the Jews. Therefore I beg you to hear me patiently.*
4 *"My manner of life from my youth, which was spent from the beginning among my own nation at Jerusalem, all the Jews know.*
5 *They knew me from the first, if they were willing to testify, that according to the strictest sect of our religion I lived a Pharisee.*
6 *And now I stand and am judged for the hope of the promise made by God to our fathers.*
7 *To this promise our twelve tribes, earnestly serving God night and day, hope to attain. For this hope's sake, King Agrippa, I am accused by the Jews.*
8 *Why should it be thought incredible by you that God raises the dead?*
9 *"Indeed, I myself thought I must do many things contrary to the name of Jesus of Nazareth.*
10 *This I also did in Jerusalem, and many of the saints I shut up in prison, having received authority from the chief priests; and when they were put to death, I cast my vote against them.*
11 *And I punished them often in every synagogue and compelled them to blaspheme; and being exceedingly enraged against them, I persecuted them even to foreign cities.*
12 *"While thus occupied, as I journeyed to Damascus with authority and commission from the chief priests,*
13 *at midday, O king, along the road I saw a light from heaven, brighter than the sun, shining around me and those who journeyed with me.*
14 *And when we all had fallen to the ground, I heard a voice speaking to me and saying in the Hebrew language, 'Saul, Saul, why are you persecuting Me? It is hard for you to kick against the goads.'*
15 *So I said, 'Who are You, Lord?' And He said, 'I am Jesus, whom you are persecuting.*
16 *But rise and stand on your feet; for I have appeared to you for this purpose, to make you a minister and a witness both of the things which you have seen and of the things which I will yet reveal to you.*
17 *I will deliver you from the Jewish people, as well as from the Gentiles, to whom I now send you,*
18 *to open their eyes, in order to turn them from darkness to light, and from the power of Satan to God, that they may receive forgiveness of sins and an inheritance among those who are sanctified by faith in Me.'*

Exploring the Meaning

4) How did Paul's encounter with the risen Christ alter his life and purpose?

5) Read Philippians 3:1–7. What about Paul's life before Christ would have caused him to see the message of Christ as "good news"?

6) What was behind Paul's eagerness to travel widely and minister to others?

Truth for Today

Some people object to terms such as *salvation* and *being saved*, claiming that the ideas they convey are out of date and meaningless to contemporary men and women. But salvation is God's term, and there is no better one to describe what He offers fallen humankind through the sacrifice of His Son. Through Christ and Christ alone, people can be saved from sin, from Satan, from judgment, from wrath, and from spiritual death.

Reflecting on the Text

7) The dying words of one ancient saint were, "Grace is the only thing that can make us like God. I might be dragged through heaven, earth, and hell and I would still be the same sinful, polluted wretch unless God Himself should cleanse me by His grace." How would you answer someone who asked: "I keep hearing about 'the grace of God.' What does that mean, and why is it such a good thing?"

8) Paul was bowled over, quite literally, by the love of God, and he never seemed to get over God's amazing grace. How can lukewarm Christians recapture a sense that the gospel is good news—the very best news ever announced?

9) Who in your life needs to hear and embrace God's good news of salvation by grace through faith in Christ? Take some time to pray for them right now.

Personal Response

Write out additional reflections, questions you may have, or a prayer.

2

The Bad News

Romans 1:18–3:20

Drawing Near

How would you respond to a sincere, concerned friend who observed: "We don't need to try to scare people into heaven with all this talk of hell, fire, and brimstone. Christians should be more positive and tolerant—emphasizing all the blessings of the Christian life, not threatening people with damnation. It just gives us—and God—a bad name!"

_____

_____

_____

The Context

After stating the thesis of his epistle—a righteous God is able to make sinners righteous through faith (1:16–17)—Paul expounds on the wretchedness of the human heart, and the divine wrath that this rebelliousness elicits.

For Paul, knowledge of eternal condemnation was one motivation he offered for coming to belief. He was determined that they understand that God is holy and just, and that we are all sinners under God's wrath. This approach makes both logical and theological sense. We cannot appreciate the wonder of God's grace and love until we truly understand God's righteous anger against sin. We cannot appreciate God's forgiveness until we appreciate the eternal consequences of sin.

Paul says that everyone—Gentiles and Jews, indeed all of humankind—stands guilty before a holy God. Human nature is corrupt. Human motives are impure. By the time Paul is finished with his divine indictment, every mouth has been shut (3:19–20). We are without excuse. We are incapable of saving ourselves. This "bad" news is a necessary part of the good news, called the gospel.

Keys to the Text

Human Depravity: The basic meaning of the Greek word, *adokimos,* "depraved," ("debased" in NKJV) is that of "not standing the test." The term was commonly used of metals that were rejected by refiners because of impurities. The impure metals were discarded, and *adokimos* therefore came to include the ideas of worthlessness and uselessness. In relation to God, the rejecting mind becomes a rejected mind and thereby becomes spiritually depraved, worthless, and useless. Because fallen humanity did not see fit to acknowledge God any longer, God gave them over, in this case here in Romans, to a depraved mind. The God-less mind is a depraved mind, whose predetermined and inevitable disposition is to do those things that are not proper. The mind that finds God worthless becomes worthless itself. It is debauched, deceived, and deserving only of God's divine wrath. Although God-less people think they are wise, they are supremely foolish (Rom. 1:22).

Divine Revelation: God testifies through Paul that all people have evidence of God, and what their physical senses can perceive of Him, their inner senses can understand to some extent. All men know something and understand something of the reality and the truth of God. They are responsible for a proper response to that revelation. Any wrong response is "inexcusable." God has made Himself known to all people everywhere in the marvels of nature and in the human conscience, which is able to distinguish right from wrong. Because this knowledge is universal and continuous, by it God has displayed His glory to everyone.

Unleashing the Text

Read 1:18–3:20, noting the key words and definitions next to the passage.

wrath of God (v. 18)—not a capricious, impulsive, arbitrary outburst of anger, but the settled determined response of a holy God against sin

manifest in them (v. 19)—God's sovereignly implanted evidence of His own existence in the heart of every person

although they knew God (v. 21)—Every person is conscious of God's existence, power, and divine nature via general revelation.

glorify (v. 21)—honor; We were created for no other reason than to exalt God, the failure or refusal to do so is the ultimate affront to our Creator.

Romans 1:18–3:20 (NKJV)

18 *For the wrath of God is revealed from heaven against all ungodliness and unrighteousness of men, who suppress the truth in unrighteousness,*

19 *because what may be known of God is manifest in them, for God has shown it to them.*

20 *For since the creation of the world His invisible attributes are clearly seen, being understood by the things that are made, even His eternal power and Godhead, so that they are without excuse,*

21 *because, although they knew God, they did not glorify Him as God, nor were thankful, but became futile in their thoughts, and their foolish hearts were darkened.*

22 *Professing to be wise, they became fools,*

23 *and changed the glory of the incorruptible God into*

an image made like corruptible man—and birds
and four-footed animals and creeping things.
24 *Therefore God also gave them up to uncleanness,*
in the lusts of their hearts, to dishonor their bodies
among themselves,
25 *who exchanged the truth of God for the lie, and*
worshiped and served the creature rather than the
Creator, who is blessed forever. Amen.
26 *For this reason God gave them up to vile passions.*
For even their women exchanged the natural use for
what is against nature.
27 *Likewise also the men, leaving the natural use of*
the woman, burned in their lust for one another,
men with men committing what is shameful, and
receiving in themselves the penalty of their error
which was due.
28 *And even as they did not like to retain God in their*
knowledge, God gave them over to a debased mind,
to do those things which are not fitting;
29 *being filled with all unrighteousness, sexual*
immorality, wickedness, covetousness,
maliciousness; full of envy, murder, strife, deceit,
evil-mindedness; they are whisperers,
30 *backbiters, haters of God, violent, proud, boasters,*
inventors of evil things, disobedient to parents,
31 *undiscerning, untrustworthy, unloving, unforgiving,*
unmerciful;
32 *who, knowing the righteous judgment of God, that*
those who practice such things are deserving of
death, not only do the same but also approve of
those who practice them.
2:1 *Therefore you are inexcusable, O man, whoever you*
are who judge, for in whatever you judge another
you condemn yourself; for you who judge practice
the same things.
2 *But we know that the judgment of God is according*
to truth against those who practice such things.
3 *And do you think this, O man, you who judge those*
practicing such things, and doing the same, that you
will escape the judgment of God?

changed the glory . . . into an image (v. 23)—the worship of idols

gave them up (vv. 24, 26)
gave them over (v. 28)—a Greek judicial term meaning to lord over a prisoner to his sentence; it conveys the sense of abandonment

the lie (v. 25)—the denying of God's existence

vile passions (v. 26)—disgraceful or degrading perversions (for example, in this context, homosexuality)

despise (2:4)—to think down on, to treat with contempt

repentance (v. 4)—the act of turning from sin to Christ for forgiveness

hardness (v. 5)—the Greek word from which we get "sclerosis," that is, a hardening of one's heart

eternal life (v. 7)—not just quantity but an endless quality of existence

partiality (v. 11)—literally, to "receive a face," that is, to give consideration to someone simply because of position, wealth, appearance, and so forth

by nature (v. 14) . . . ***conscience*** (v. 15)—our God-given instinctive or innate sense of what is right and wrong

4 *Or do you despise the riches of His goodness,*
forbearance, and longsuffering, not knowing that
the goodness of God leads you to repentance?
5 *But in accordance with your hardness and your*
impenitent heart you are treasuring up for yourself
wrath in the day of wrath and revelation of the
righteous judgment of God,
6 *who "will render to each one according to his*
deeds":
7 *eternal life to those who by patient continuance in*
doing good seek for glory, honor, and immortality;
8 *but to those who are self-seeking and do not obey*
the truth, but obey unrighteousness—indignation
and wrath,
9 *tribulation and anguish, on every soul of man who*
does evil, of the Jew first and also of the Greek;
10 *but glory, honor, and peace to everyone who works*
what is good, to the Jew first and also to the Greek.
11 *For there is no partiality with God.*
12 *For as many as have sinned without law will also*
perish without law, and as many as have sinned in
the law will be judged by the law
13 *(for not the hearers of the law are just in the sight of*
God, but the doers of the law will be justified;
14 *for when Gentiles, who do not have the law, by*
nature do the things in the law, these, although not
having the law, are a law to themselves,
15 *who show the work of the law written in their*
hearts, their conscience also bearing witness, and
between themselves their thoughts accusing or else
excusing them)
16 *in the day when God will judge the secrets of men by*
Jesus Christ, according to my gospel.
17 *Indeed you are called a Jew, and rest on the law, and*
make your boast in God,
18 *and know His will, and approve the things that are*
excellent, being instructed out of the law,
19 *and are confident that you yourself are a guide to*
the blind, a light to those who are in darkness,

20 *an instructor of the foolish, a teacher of babes,*
having the form of knowledge and truth in the law.
21 *You, therefore, who teach another, do you not teach*
yourself? You who preach that a man should not
steal, do you steal?
22 *You who say, "Do not commit adultery," do you*
commit adultery? You who abhor idols, do you rob
temples?
23 *You who make your boast in the law, do you*
dishonor God through breaking the law?
24 *For "the name of God is blasphemed among the*
Gentiles because of you," as it is written.
25 *For circumcision is indeed profitable if you keep*
the law; but if you are a breaker of the law, your
circumcision has become uncircumcision.
26 *Therefore, if an uncircumcised man keeps the*
righteous requirements of the law, will not his
uncircumcision be counted as circumcision?
27 *And will not the physically uncircumcised, if he*
fulfills the law, judge you who, even with your
written code and circumcision, are a transgressor of
the law?
28 *For he is not a Jew who is one outwardly, nor is*
circumcision that which is outward in the flesh;
29 *but he is a Jew who is one inwardly; and*
circumcision is that of the heart, in the Spirit, not
in the letter; whose praise is not from men but from
God.
3:1 *What advantage then has the Jew, or what is the*
profit of circumcision?
2 *Much in every way! Chiefly because to them were*
committed the oracles of God.
3 *For what if some did not believe? Will their*
unbelief make the faithfulness of God without
effect?
4 *Certainly not! Indeed, let God be true but every*
man a liar. As it is written: "That You may be
justified in Your words, And may overcome when
You are judged."

he is a Jew (v. 29)—The true child of God has a heart separated from sin unto God.

oracles (3:2)—important supernatural sayings or messages

I speak as a man (v. 5)—Paul is paraphrasing the weak, unbiblical logic of his opponents.

we (v. 9)—the Christians in Rome

under sin (v. 9)—enslaved and dominated by sin

unprofitable (v. 12)—useless, worthless; the Hebrew equivalent was used to describe milk that had become rancid

cursing (v. 14)—caustically, derisively wishing the worst for someone

every mouth may be stopped (v. 19)—People are silent and speechless before God's righteous judgment.

5 *But if our unrighteousness demonstrates the*
righteousness of God, what shall we say? Is God
unjust who inflicts wrath? (I speak as a man.)
6 *Certainly not! For then how will God judge the*
world?
7 *For if the truth of God has increased through my lie*
to His glory, why am I also still judged as a sinner?
8 *And why not say, "Let us do evil that good may*
come"?—as we are slanderously reported and as
some affirm that we say. Their condemnation is
just.
9 *What then? Are we better than they? Not at all. For*
we have previously charged both Jews and Greeks
that they are all under sin.
10 *As it is written: "There is none righteous, no, not*
one;
11 *There is none who understands; There is none who*
seeks after God.
12 *They have all turned aside; They have together*
become unprofitable; There is none who does good,
no, not one."
13 *"Their throat is an open tomb; With their tongues*
they have practiced deceit"; "The poison of asps is
under their lips";
14 *"Whose mouth is full of cursing and bitterness."*
15 *"Their feet are swift to shed blood;*
16 *Destruction and misery are in their ways;*
17 *And the way of peace they have not known."*
18 *"There is no fear of God before their eyes."*
19 *Now we know that whatever the law says, it says to*
those who are under the law, that every mouth may
be stopped, and all the world may become guilty
before God.
20 *Therefore by the deeds of the law no flesh will be*
justified in His sight, for by the law is the knowledge
of sin.

1) What reasons does Paul give for the wrath of God against humanity?

_____

_____

_____

2) Circle all the words and descriptive phrases in this passage for man's rebellion against God.

3) Other than long-term judgment, what short-term consequences of rebelliousness does Paul cite in this extended passage?

_____

_____

_____

4) According to this passage, why are not even "moral" and religious people exempted from God's widespread judgment?

_____

_____

_____

Going Deeper

Read Psalm 14 and note how it relates to the above passage in Romans.

Psalm 14 (NKJV)

1 *The fool has said in his heart, "There is no God." They are corrupt, They have done abominable works, There is none who does good.*
2 *The* LORD *looks down from heaven upon the children of men, To see if there are any who understand, who seek God.*
3 *They have all turned aside, They have together become corrupt; There is none who does good, No, not one.*
4 *Have all the workers of iniquity no knowledge, Who eat up my people as they eat bread, And do not call on the* LORD*?*
5 *There they are in great fear, For God is with the generation of the righteous.*
6 *You shame the counsel of the poor, But the* LORD *is his refuge.*
7 *Oh, that the salvation of Israel would come out of Zion! When the* LORD *brings back the captivity of His people, Let Jacob rejoice and Israel be glad.*

Exploring the Meaning

5) How do these passages from both Old and New Testaments answer the popular, modern-day belief that "human beings are basically good"?

6) What specific evidence do you see in this passage to suggest that God is not impressed by mere "religious activity"?

7) Read Galatians 3:19–25. Why did God give sinful human beings a perfect law code to follow?

Truth for Today

The final verdict, then, is that unredeemed humankind has no defense whatever and is guilty of all charges. The defense must rest, as it were, before it has opportunity to say anything, because the omniscient and all-wise God has infallibly demonstrated the impossibility of any grounds for acquittal. Absolute silence is the only possible response just as there will be utter silence in heaven when the Lord Jesus Christ will one day break the seventh seal and release the seven trumpet judgments upon the condemned earth (see Rev. 8:1–6).

Reflecting on the Text

8) R. A. Torrey observed: "When we see sin in all its hideousness and enormity, the holiness of God in all its perfection, and the glory of Jesus Christ in all its infinity, nothing but a doctrine that those who persist in . . . the rejection of the Son of God shall endure everlasting anguish will satisfy the demands of our own moral intuitions." How can you come to a deeper understanding of the depravity of the human heart and the holiness of our God?

9) What in this study convicts you most? challenges you most? compels you to action the most? Why?

Personal Response

Write out additional reflections, questions you may have, or a prayer.

Additional Notes

3

By Faith Alone

Romans 3:21–4:25

Drawing Near

What does *faith* mean to you? How would you explain it to a child?

_____

_____

_____

_____

The Context

In Homer's *Iliad*, the great Trojan warrior, Hector, was preparing to fight Achilles and the invading Greeks. As he was about to leave home, Hector wanted to hold his young son Astayanax in his arms and bid him farewell. But Hector's armor so frightened the infant that he shrank back to his nurse's caress. The father, laughing out loud, then removed his bronze helmet and took up his little child in his arms. The boy discovered his loving father behind all that armor.

That is similar to what Paul does here in Romans. Having shown God as holy judge, he now shows the God of love, who reaches out with open arms to sinful people in the hope that they will come to Him and be saved. After conclusively proving the universal sinfulness of humanity and their desperate need for righteousness (1:18–3:20), Paul shifts gears and demonstrates that God alone can provide that righteousness. To illustrate this truth, Paul devotes the entire fourth chapter to Abraham. This godly Old Testament saint is a shining example of the central biblical truth that a person can become right with God only by faith in response to His grace, never by works.

Keys to the Text

Justification: The words *justify* and *justification* occur some thirty times in Romans and are concentrated in 2:13–5:1. This legal or forensic term comes from the Greek word for "righteous" and means "to declare righteous." This verdict includes: pardon from the guilt and penalty of sin, and the imputation of Christ's righteousness to the believer's account, which provides for the positive righteousness man needs to be accepted by God. God declares a sinner righteous solely on the basis of the merits of Christ's righteousness. God imputed a believer's sin to Christ's account in His sacrificial death. The sinner receives this gift of God's grace by faith alone. Justification is a gracious gift God extends to the repentant, believing sinner, wholly apart from human merit or work.

Abraham: Paul uses the model of Abraham to prove justification by faith alone because the Jews held him up as the supreme example of a righteous man (John 8:39), and because it clearly showed that Judaism with its works-righteousness had deviated from the faith of the Jews' patriarchal ancestors. In a spiritual sense, Abraham was the forerunner of the primarily Gentile church in Rome, as well.

Unleashing the Text

Read 3:21–4:25, noting the key words and definitions next to the passage.

But (v. 21)—an adversative, contrasting humanity's total depravity and inability to please God, and God's own provision of a way to Himself

propitiation (v. 25)—appeasement or satisfaction; Christ's death satisfied the offended holiness of God

passed over (v. 25)—a temporary withholding of judgment

Romans 3:21–4:25 (NKJV)

21 *But now the righteousness of God apart from the law is revealed, being witnessed by the Law and the Prophets,*
22 *even the righteousness of God, through faith in Jesus Christ, to all and on all who believe. For there is no difference;*
23 *for all have sinned and fall short of the glory of God,*
24 *being justified freely by His grace through the redemption that is in Christ Jesus,*
25 *whom God set forth as a propitiation by His blood, through faith, to demonstrate His righteousness, because in His forbearance God had passed over the sins that were previously committed,*
26 *to demonstrate at the present time His righteousness, that He might be just and the justifier of the one who has faith in Jesus.*
27 *Where is boasting then? It is excluded. By what law? Of works? No, but by the law of faith.*
28 *Therefore we conclude that a man is justified by faith apart from the deeds of the law.*
29 *Or is He the God of the Jews only? Is He not also the God of the Gentiles? Yes, of the Gentiles also,*
30 *since there is one God who will justify the circumcised by faith and the uncircumcised through faith.*

31 *Do we then make void the law through faith?*
Certainly not! On the contrary, we establish the
law.
4:1 *What then shall we say that Abraham our father*
has found according to the flesh?
2 *For if Abraham was justified by works, he has*
something to boast about, but not before God.
3 *For what does the Scripture say? "Abraham*
believed God, and it was accounted to him for
righteousness."
4 *Now to him who works, the wages are not counted*
as grace but as debt.
5 *But to him who does not work but believes on Him*
who justifies the ungodly, his faith is accounted for
righteousness,
6 *just as David also describes the blessedness of the*
man to whom God imputes righteousness apart
from works:
7 *"Blessed are those whose lawless deeds are forgiven,*
And whose sins are covered;
8 *Blessed is the man to whom the Lord shall not*
impute sin."
9 *Does this blessedness then come upon the*
circumcised only, or upon the uncircumcised also?
For we say that faith was accounted to Abraham for
righteousness.
10 *How then was it accounted? While he was*
circumcised, or uncircumcised? Not while
circumcised, but while uncircumcised.
11 *And he received the sign of circumcision, a seal*
of the righteousness of the faith which he had
while still uncircumcised, that he might be the
father of all those who believe, though they are
uncircumcised, that righteousness might be imputed
to them also,
12 *and the father of circumcision to those who not only*
are of the circumcision, but who also walk in the
steps of the faith which our father Abraham had
while still uncircumcised.

accounted (4:3)—a word used in legal and financial settings; here to take something that belongs to someone and credit it to the account of another

justifies the ungodly (v. 5)—Only those who freely admit their unworthiness are candidates for salvation.

David (v. 6)—King David's sin with Bathsheba is another Old Testament example of imputed righteousness.

the sign of circumcision (v. 11)—the physical, racial mark of identity for the Jewish people

walk in the steps (v. 12)—those non-Jews who emulate Abraham's faith

faith is made void and the promise made of no effect (v. 14)—Paul is demonstrating that if adherence to the Law could save, then faith in God's promise would be worthless.

weak in faith (v. 19)—to allow doubt to erode and undermine belief

delivered up (v. 25)—to be crucified as punishment for human beings' sins

13 *For the promise that he would be the heir of the world was not to Abraham or to his seed through the law, but through the righteousness of faith.*
14 *For if those who are of the law are heirs, faith is made void and the promise made of no effect,*
15 *because the law brings about wrath; for where there is no law there is no transgression.*
16 *Therefore it is of faith that it might be according to grace, so that the promise might be sure to all the seed, not only to those who are of the law, but also to those who are of the faith of Abraham, who is the father of us all*
17 *(as it is written, "I have made you a father of many nations") in the presence of Him whom he believed—God, who gives life to the dead and calls those things which do not exist as though they did;*
18 *who, contrary to hope, in hope believed, so that he became the father of many nations, according to what was spoken, "So shall your descendants be."*
19 *And not being weak in faith, he did not consider his own body, already dead (since he was about a hundred years old), and the deadness of Sarah's womb.*
20 *He did not waver at the promise of God through unbelief, but was strengthened in faith, giving glory to God,*
21 *and being fully convinced that what He had promised He was also able to perform.*
22 *And therefore "it was accounted to him for righteousness."*
23 *Now it was not written for his sake alone that it was imputed to him,*
24 *but also for us. It shall be imputed to us who believe in Him who raised up Jesus our Lord from the dead,*
25 *who was delivered up because of our offenses, and was raised because of our justification.*

1) Why does Paul argue that when it comes to one's standing before God, no one has the right to boast or be filled with religious pride?

2) Circle every word or phrase in this passage that describes what God has done.

3) Paul goes to some lengths to demonstrate that Abraham was justified in the sight of God long before he was ever circumcised. Why was this an important argument for him to make to his Roman audience?

4) Underline every reference in the passage to God's law. What is the purpose or effect of God's law (4:13–15)?

Going Deeper

Read Galatians 3:6–25, noting the parallels with Romans 3:21–4:25.

Galatians 3:6–25 (NKJV)

6 *just as Abraham "believed God, and it was accounted to him for righteousness."*
7 *Therefore know that only those who are of faith are sons of Abraham.*
8 *And the Scripture, foreseeing that God would justify the Gentiles by faith, preached the gospel to Abraham beforehand, saying, "In you all the nations shall be blessed."*

9 *So then those who are of faith are blessed with believing Abraham.*
10 *For as many as are of the works of the law are under the curse; for it is written, "Cursed is everyone who does not continue in all things which are written in the book of the law, to do them."*
11 *But that no one is justified by the law in the sight of God is evident, for "the just shall live by faith."*
12 *Yet the law is not of faith, but "the man who does them shall live by them."*
13 *Christ has redeemed us from the curse of the law, having become a curse for us (for it is written, "Cursed is everyone who hangs on a tree"),*
14 *that the blessing of Abraham might come upon the Gentiles in Christ Jesus, that we might receive the promise of the Spirit through faith.*
15 *Brethren, I speak in the manner of men: Though it is only a man's covenant, yet if it is confirmed, no one annuls or adds to it.*
16 *Now to Abraham and his Seed were the promises made. He does not say, "And to seeds," as of many, but as of one, "And to your Seed," who is Christ.*
17 *And this I say, that the law, which was four hundred and thirty years later, cannot annul the covenant that was confirmed before by God in Christ, that it should make the promise of no effect.*
18 *For if the inheritance is of the law, it is no longer of promise; but God gave it to Abraham by promise.*
19 *What purpose then does the law serve? It was added because of transgressions, till the Seed should come to whom the promise was made; and it was appointed through angels by the hand of a mediator.*
20 *Now a mediator does not mediate for one only, but God is one.*
21 *Is the law then against the promises of God? Certainly not! For if there had been a law given which could have given life, truly righteousness would have been by the law.*
22 *But the Scripture has confined all under sin, that the promise by faith in Jesus Christ might be given to those who believe.*
23 *But before faith came, we were kept under guard by the law, kept for the faith which would afterward be revealed.*
24 *Therefore the law was our tutor to bring us to Christ, that we might be justified by faith.*
25 *But after faith has come, we are no longer under a tutor.*

Exploring the Meaning

5) What points in Galatians 3 underscore Paul's argument in Romans 3–4?

6) What incidents from the life of Abraham and Sarah does Paul use to make the case that salvation is by divine power, not human effort?

7) Read 2 Corinthians 5:21. If God's wrath is directed toward unrighteousness, and His favor is directed toward righteousness, what are the wonderful implications of this verse for believers?

Truth for Today

Scripture makes it clear that there is indeed a way to God, but that it is not based on anything men can do to achieve or merit it. Man can be made right with God, but not on his own terms or in his own power. In that basic regard Christianity is distinct from every other religion. As far as the way of salvation is concerned, there are therefore only two religions the world has ever known or will ever know—the religion of divine accomplishment, which is biblical Christianity, and the religion of human achievement, which includes all other kinds of religion, by whatever names they may claim.

Reflecting on the Text

8) Some Christians view God's law and His grace as contradictory. Based on what you have seen in this study, how would you harmonize these two truths?

9) What's the problem with trying to *do* things in order to earn favor with God? Why is that never sufficient?

10) If salvation were by human effort, we could boast. Since salvation is all of grace, what is the proper response of the redeemed?

Personal Response

Write out additional reflections, questions you may have, or a prayer.

Additional Notes

4

Grace through One Man

Romans 5:1–21

Drawing Near

Have you ever experienced doubts about your salvation? In what way?

_____

_____

_____

Why is it sometimes hard to believe that you are secure in Christ forever?

_____

_____

_____

The Context

After describing the appalling sin and lostness of all humankind, Paul revealed how Christ, by His death on the cross, has provided the way of salvation for everyone who comes to God in faith. Next, Paul moves to answer two important questions that were, no doubt, on the minds of his readers. First, how complete, or how secure is this salvation provided by Christ? Can we really be certain? What happens if we sin after turning to Christ in faith? Paul addresses this query in 5:1–11.

The second issue addressed here by Paul is, "How can what one man did at one time in history have such an absolute effect on humankind?" Paul concisely answers this question by comparing the reign of death that Adam's sin engendered with the reign of life made possible by Christ's perfect sacrifice. Though many people consider the latter half of Romans 5 to be one of the most enigmatic passages in the New Testament, when looked at carefully, this chapter is a source of great comfort and genuine awe in a God who is able and willing to provide such an extraordinary salvation.

Keys to the Text

Imputed: Used in both financial and legal settings, the Greek word means to take something that belongs to someone and credit to another's account. It is a one-sided transaction. As in the case of Abraham, Abraham did nothing to accumulate it; God simply credited it to him. God took His own righteousness and credited it to Abraham as if it were actually his. God did this because Abraham believed in Him. This is the heart of the doctrine of justification, whereby God declares the repentant sinner righteous the moment he places wholehearted faith in Christ and His sacrificial death. Christ made atonement by shedding His own blood on the cross. This provides forgiveness. And just as our sins were put to His account when He bore them on the cross, so now His righteousness is reckoned as our own. His perfect righteousness thus becomes the ground on which we stand before God.

Types: A figure, representation, or symbol of something to come, as an event in the Old Testament foreshadows another in the New Testament. Types generally find their fulfillment in the person and ministry of Christ, but they sometimes relate to God, His people, or some other reality. For instance, Melchizedek, the king-priest of Salem (Gen. 14:18–20 and Ps. 110:4), is said to be typical of Christ (Heb. 6:20). Jesus said the bronze serpent in the wilderness (Num. 21:4–9) was in some sense typical of His own crucifixion (John 3:14–15). The writer of Hebrews (Heb. 9–10) pointed out that the tabernacle typically foreshadowed the person and work of Jesus Christ. The NKJV uses the word "type" in Romans 5:14, where Paul mentions Adam as "a type of Him [Jesus] who was to come." (*Nelson's New Illustrated Bible Dictionary*)

Unleashing the Text

Read 5:1–21, noting the key words and definitions next to the passage.

Romans 5:1–21 (NKJV)

1 *Therefore, having been justified by faith, we have peace with God through our Lord Jesus Christ,*
2 *through whom also we have access by faith into this grace in which we stand, and rejoice in hope of the glory of God.*
3 *And not only that, but we also glory in tribulations, knowing that tribulation produces perseverance;*
4 *and perseverance, character; and character, hope.*
5 *Now hope does not disappoint, because the love of God has been poured out in our hearts by the Holy Spirit who was given to us.*
6 *For when we were still without strength, in due time Christ died for the ungodly.*

having been justified (v. 1)—The Greek construction of this verb indicates a one-time legal declaration with ongoing results.

we have (v. 1)—we presently possess

peace with God (v. 1)—an external, objective reality, not a subjective, internal sense of serenity and calm

access (v. 2)—introduction

stand (v. 2)—the idea of permanence, of being fixed and immovable

7 *For scarcely for a righteous man will one die; yet perhaps for a good man someone would even dare to die.*

8 *But God demonstrates His own love toward us, in that while we were still sinners, Christ died for us.*

9 *Much more then, having now been justified by His blood, we shall be saved from wrath through Him.*

10 *For if when we were enemies we were reconciled to God through the death of His Son, much more, having been reconciled, we shall be saved by His life.*

11 *And not only that, but we also rejoice in God through our Lord Jesus Christ, through whom we have now received the reconciliation.*

12 *Therefore, just as through one man sin entered the world, and death through sin, and thus death spread to all men, because all sinned—*

13 *(For until the law sin was in the world, but sin is not imputed when there is no law.*

14 *Nevertheless death reigned from Adam to Moses, even over those who had not sinned according to the likeness of the transgression of Adam, who is a type of Him who was to come.*

15 *But the free gift is not like the offense. For if by the one man's offense many died, much more the grace of God and the gift by the grace of the one Man, Jesus Christ, abounded to many.*

16 *And the gift is not like that which came through the one who sinned. For the judgment which came from one offense resulted in condemnation, but the free gift which came from many offenses resulted in justification.*

17 *For if by the one man's offense death reigned through the one, much more those who receive abundance of grace and of the gift of righteousness will reign in life through the One, Jesus Christ.)*

18 *Therefore, as through one man's offense judgment came to all men, resulting in condemnation, even so through one Man's righteous act the free gift came to all men, resulting in justification of life.*

hope (v. 2)—a certainty not yet realized; not a wishful, uncertain dream

tribulations (v. 3)—extreme pressure, as in the pressure exerted to extract oil from an olive

perseverance (v. 4)—remaining under tremendous weight without succumbing; endurance

character (v. 4)—literally "proof," a term used in the testing of precious metals to determine their purity

poured out (v. 5)—God's love is lavished on His children.

without strength (v. 6)—literally "helpless," because of their spiritual deadness

ungodly (v. 6)—a proof that Christ's love was never based on human merit

because all sinned (v. 12)—All humanity existed in the loins of Adam and have through procreation inherited his fallenness and depravity. Thus it can be said that all sinned in him.

a type of Him . . . to come (v. 14)—Adam and Christ were similar in that their acts affected many others.

death reigned (v. 17)—Adam's sinful act brought universal death.

19 *For as by one man's disobedience many were made sinners, so also by one Man's obedience many will be made righteous.*
20 *Moreover the law entered that the offense might abound. But where sin abounded, grace abounded much more,*
21 *so that as sin reigned in death, even so grace might reign through righteousness to eternal life through Jesus Christ our Lord.*

1) Circle all the verbs in verses 1–11, noting especially their tenses.

2) How does Paul refute the erroneous notion that we receive salvation by faith but must preserve it by good works? What evidences does he give that salvation is unconditional?

3) What word picture does Paul use to drive home the truth that unbelievers are actually at war with God?

4) How did Adam's actions affect the human race? What were the effects of Christ's actions?

Going Deeper

Read the following passage and consider what the author has to say about the law's inability to save us, Christ's perfect sacrifice, and the possibilities this creates for relating to God.

Hebrews 10:1–4, 12–14, 19–23 (NKJV)

1 *For the law, having a shadow of the good things to come, and not the very image of the things, can never with these same sacrifices, which they offer continually year by year, make those who approach perfect.*
2 *For then would they not have ceased to be offered? For the worshipers, once purified, would have had no more consciousness of sins.*
3 *But in those sacrifices there is a reminder of sins every year.*
4 *For it is not possible that the blood of bulls and goats could take away sins.*
12 *But this Man, after He had offered one sacrifice for sins forever, sat down at the right hand of God,*
13 *from that time waiting till His enemies are made His footstool.*
14 *For by one offering He has perfected forever those who are being sanctified.*
19 *Therefore, brethren, having boldness to enter the Holiest by the blood of Jesus,*
20 *by a new and living way which He consecrated for us, through the veil, that is, His flesh,*
21 *and having a High Priest over the house of God,*
22 *let us draw near with a true heart in full assurance of faith, having our hearts sprinkled from an evil conscience and our bodies washed with pure water.*
23 *Let us hold fast the confession of our hope without wavering, for He who promised is faithful.*

Exploring the Meaning

5) In what way was Jesus's sacrifice different from the old sacrificial system?

_____

_____

_____

_____

_____

6) Why do you think both of these passages (Romans 4; Hebrews 10) emphasize our access to God?

7) In what ways does this Hebrews passage echo the idea that salvation is permanent?

Truth for Today

Jesus Christ broke the power of sin and death, but the converse is not true. Sin and death cannot break the power of Jesus Christ. The condemnation of Adam's sin is reversible, the redemption of Jesus Christ is not. The effect of Adam's act is permanent only if not nullified by Christ. The effect of Christ's act, however, is permanent for believing individuals and not subject to reversal or nullification. We have the great assurance that once we are in Jesus Christ, we are in Him forever.

Reflecting on the Text

8) A. W. Pink said the following about our eternal security in Christ: "It is utterly and absolutely impossible that the sentence of the divine Judge should ever be revoked or reversed. Sooner shall the lightnings of omnipotence shiver the Rock of Ages than those sheltering in Him again be brought under condemnation." How does knowing that your salvation is eternally secure affect your life on a daily basis? How does it make you feel?

9) When have you experienced God's love being "poured out" (v. 5)?

10) What new things about God have you learned from this passage?

Personal Response

Write out additional reflections, questions you may have, or a prayer.

Additional Notes

5

Dead and Alive!

Romans 6:1–23

Drawing Near

Think of an area in which you have struggled with sin in your life. How has God helped you overcome these struggles?

_____

_____

_____

The Context

Like a skillful lawyer building an airtight case, the apostle Paul has been laying out the remarkable facts of the gospel. After an extensive discussion of human beings' sin and inability to please God, Paul announced the doctrine of justification, which is God's declaration of believing sinners as righteous. Next he moves to the subject of the believer's *holiness*—living in obedience to God's Word through the power of His Spirit. In short, Paul sets out to demonstrate the practical ramifications of salvation for those who have been justified. He specifically begins a lengthy discussion on the doctrine of sanctification, which is the process of becoming holy.

Paul also addresses the logical conclusion of his readers: If the old self is dead, why is there continually a struggle with sin, and how can the new self become dominant? His exhortation is contained in two key words: *reckon* (vv. 11b–12) and *present* (vv. 13–14). The final section of chapter 6 continues Paul's discussion of sanctification by reminding his readers of their past slavery to sin and their new slavery to righteousness. He wants them to live in submission to their new master, Jesus Christ, and not to be entangled again with the sins that characterized their old life, sins which no longer have any claim over them.

Keys to the Text

To Reckon: While it literally means "to count or number something," this phrase was often used metaphorically to refer to having an absolute, unreserved confidence in what one's mind knows to be true—the kind of heartfelt confidence that affects his actions and decisions. Paul is not referring to mind games in which we trick ourselves into thinking a certain way. Rather he is urging us to embrace by faith what God has revealed to be true.

Dead to Sin: Not a reference to the believer's ongoing daily struggle with sin, but to a one-time event completed in the past. Because we are "in Christ" (Rom. 6:11; 8:1) and He died in our place (5:6–8), we are counted dead with Him. This is the fundamental premise of chapter 6, and Paul spends the remainder of the chapter explaining and supporting it.

Not Under Law But Under Grace (6:14). This does not mean God has abrogated His moral law. The law is good, holy, and righteous; but it cannot be kept, so it curses. Since it cannot assist anyone to keep God's moral standard (see Rom. 7:7–11), it can only show the standard and thus rebuke and condemn those who fail to keep it. But the believer is no longer under the law as a condition of acceptance with God—an impossible condition to meet and one designed only to show man his sinfulness—but under grace, which enables him to truly fulfill the law's righteous requirements. See chapter 7 for Paul's complete commentary on this crucial expression.

Unleashing the Text

Read 6:1–23, noting the key words and definitions next to the passage.

Romans 6:1–23 (NKJV)

1 *What shall we say then? Shall we continue in sin that grace may abound?*
2 *Certainly not! How shall we who died to sin live any longer in it?*
3 *Or do you not know that as many of us as were baptized into Christ Jesus were baptized into His death?*
4 *Therefore we were buried with Him through baptism into death, that just as Christ was raised from the dead by the glory of the Father, even so we also should walk in newness of life.*
5 *For if we have been united together in the likeness of His death, certainly we also shall be in the likeness of His resurrection,*
6 *knowing this, that our old man was crucified with Him, that the body of sin might be done away with, that we should no longer be slaves of sin.*
7 *For he who has died has been freed from sin.*
8 *Now if we died with Christ, we believe that we shall also live with Him,*

Shall we continue in sin . . . (v. 1)—Paul anticipated that skeptics might reason, "If salvation is based entirely upon grace, won't this encourage them to sin even more?"

Certainly not! (v. 2)—literally, "may it never be, by no means"; a strong Greek idiom of repudiation

baptized into Christ Jesus (v. 3)—Not a literal water baptism, but a metaphorical immersion of a person into the work of Christ; that is, completely united and identified with Him, "so as to alter [a person's] condition or relationship to [his or her] previous environment or condition" (Wuest).

newness of life (v. 4)—In the same way that we were united with Christ in His death and burial, so too in His resurrection; this speaks of regeneration.

our old man (v. 6)—a believer's unregenerate self, worn out and useless

9 *knowing that Christ, having been raised from the dead, dies no more. Death no longer has dominion over Him.*
10 *For the death that He died, He died to sin once for all; but the life that He lives, He lives to God.*
11 *Likewise you also, reckon yourselves to be dead indeed to sin, but alive to God in Christ Jesus our Lord.*
12 *Therefore do not let sin reign in your mortal body, that you should obey it in its lusts.*
13 *And do not present your members as instruments of unrighteousness to sin, but present yourselves to God as being alive from the dead, and your members as instruments of righteousness to God.*
14 *For sin shall not have dominion over you, for you are not under law but under grace.*
15 *What then? Shall we sin because we are not under law but under grace? Certainly not!*
16 *Do you not know that to whom you present yourselves slaves to obey, you are that one's slaves whom you obey, whether of sin leading to death, or of obedience leading to righteousness?*
17 *But God be thanked that though you were slaves of sin, yet you obeyed from the heart that form of doctrine to which you were delivered.*
18 *And having been set free from sin, you became slaves of righteousness.*
19 *I speak in human terms because of the weakness of your flesh. For just as you presented your members as slaves of uncleanness, and of lawlessness leading to more lawlessness, so now present your members as slaves of righteousness for holiness.*
20 *For when you were slaves of sin, you were free in regard to righteousness.*
21 *What fruit did you have then in the things of which you are now ashamed? For the end of those things is death.*
22 *But now having been set free from sin, and having become slaves of God, you have your fruit to holiness, and the end, everlasting life.*
23 *For the wages of sin is death, but the gift of God is eternal life in Christ Jesus our Lord.*

crucified (v. 6)—not merely made to suffer but put to death

body of sin (v. 6)—essentially a synonym for the "old man"

freed from sin (v. 7)—no longer under sin's domination

dominion (v. 9)—mastery, control, or domination

mortal body (v. 12)—the only remaining repository where sin finds the believer vulnerable

present (v. 13)—refers to a decision of the will

your members (v. 13)—the parts of the physical body from which sin operates in the life of a believer

weakness of your flesh (v. 19)—the human difficulty in grasping divine truth

1) How would you summarize Paul's response to the idea that believers in Christ will continue to live as they did when they were unbelievers?

2) What does Paul say happened to our old selves?

3) What things do believers need to "know"? How does this "knowing" differ from the "reckoning" (v. 11) that believers are commanded to do?

4) What three things are part of the process of sanctification (vv. 6, 11, 13)?

Going Deeper

Note the parallels in Colossians 3 with what you've been studying in chapter 6.

Colossians 3:1–11

1 *If then you were raised with Christ, seek those things which are above,*
where Christ is, sitting at the right hand of God.
2 *Set your mind on things above, not on things on the earth.*
3 *For you died, and your life is hidden with Christ in God.*
4 *When Christ who is our life appears, then you also will appear with Him*
in glory.
5 *Therefore put to death your members which are on the earth: fornication,*
uncleanness, passion, evil desire, and covetousness, which is idolatry.
6 *Because of these things the wrath of God is coming upon the sons of*
disobedience,
7 *in which you yourselves once walked when you lived in them.*
8 *But now you yourselves are to put off all these: anger, wrath, malice,*
blasphemy, filthy language out of your mouth.
9 *Do not lie to one another, since you have put off the old man with his*
deeds,
10 *and have put on the new man who is renewed in knowledge according to*
the image of Him who created him,
11 *where there is neither Greek nor Jew, circumcised nor uncircumcised,*
barbarian, Scythian, slave nor free, but Christ is all and in all.

Exploring the Meaning

5) Why are Christians to "put off" and "put on" certain things?

_____

_____

_____

_____

_____

6) If Christians really are dead to sin and alive to God, why do we still struggle so with temptation?

_____

_____

_____

_____

7) These passages teach two truths: (1) *God* is the One who changes us—sanctification is by His grace; and (2) in the sanctification process *we* are to do certain things and not do certain things. How do you reconcile these facts?

Truth for Today

Jesus Christ is not looking for people who want to add Him to their life as an insurance against hell. He is not looking for people who want to apply His high moral principles to their unregenerate lives. He is not looking for those who want only to be outwardly reformed by having their old nature improved. Jesus Christ calls to Himself those who are willing to be inwardly transformed by Him, who desire an entirely new nature that is created in His own holy likeness. He calls to Himself those who are willing to die with Him in order to be raised with Him, who are willing to relinquish slavery to their sin for slavery to His righteousness. And when people come to Him on His terms, He changes their destiny from eternal death to eternal life.

Reflecting on the Text

8) What do you think it means to come to Jesus "on His own terms"? Are you willing to relinquish your sinful inclinations and be transformed from the inside out?

9) The noble theologian Charles Hodge summarized: "There can be no participation in Christ's life without a participation in his death, and we cannot enjoy the benefits of his death unless we are partakers of the power of his life. We must be reconciled to God in order to be holy, and we cannot be reconciled without thereby becoming holy." What are some barriers in your life to becoming holy? What are some things in your life that contribute to becoming more holy?

10) In the three-part process of sanctification described in this passage (that is, "know," "reckon," and "present"), in what area do you struggle the most? Is it in understanding God's salvation truths and really being convinced by them, or choosing to live them out? Explain.

Personal Response

Write out additional reflections, questions you may have, or a prayer.

Additional Notes

6

Delivered from the Law

Romans 7:1–25

Drawing Near

Would you describe yourself as a rigid "rule keeper"? Why or why not?

_____

_____

_____

Ask God to show you new truths in this study about His power over sin and His love for you.

The Context

In this doctrinal masterpiece, Paul, the consummate theologian, has first established the sad, sinful state of human beings. All are under *condemnation*. However, the good news includes the miracle of *justification*—a righteousness from God available by grace through faith. But the gospel received from God and preached by Paul doesn't stop there. It also includes *sanctification*—that truth of absolute identification with Christ (in His death, burial, and resurrection), by which God transforms redeemed sinners into the very likeness of Christ.

Knowing that his readers—especially Jewish ones—would have many questions about how the Old Testament laws relate to their faith in Christ, Paul sets out to explain that law convicts unbelievers (and believers) of sin, but it cannot deliver anyone from sin. He also addresses the issue of why believers still struggle with sinful desires.

Keys to the Text

The Law: In the Bible, particularly the Old Testament, a unique law code was established by direct revelation from God to direct His people in their worship, in their relationship to Him, and in their social relationships with one another. Israel was not the only nation to have a law code. Such collections were common among the countries of the ancient world. The biblical law code, or the Mosaic Law, was different from other ancient Near Eastern law codes in several ways. Biblical law was different, first of all, in its origin. Throughout the ancient world, the laws of most nations were believed to originate with the gods, but they were considered intensely personal and subjective in the way they were applied. By contrast, the biblical concept was that law comes from God, issues from His nature, and is holy, righteous, and good. Furthermore, at the outset of God's ruling over Israel at Sinai, God the great King gave His laws. These laws were binding on His people, and He upheld them. Furthermore, His laws were universal and an expression of His love for His people (Exod. 19:5–6). If salvation has always been by faith and never by works, and if the covenant of promise to Abraham was fulfilled in Jesus Christ, what purpose did the Law have? Paul's answer is direct and sobering: The purpose of the Law was to demonstrate to man his total sinfulness, his inability to please God by his own works, and his need for mercy and grace. (*Nelson's New Illustrated Bible Dictionary*)

Unleashing the Text

Read 7:1–25, noting the key words and definitions next to the passage.

dominion (v. 1)—jurisdiction

become dead (v. 4)—literally "you were made to die"; in response to a sinner's faith, God makes the sinner forever dead to the condemnation and penalty of law

married to another (v. 4)—united with Christ in a permanent relationship

fruit (v. 4)—a transformed life that manifests new attitudes and actions

flesh (v. 5)—people's unredeemed humanness, that is, that remnant of the old man that will remain with each believer until each receives his or her glorified body

sinful passions (v. 5)—the overwhelming impulses to think and do evil

aroused by the law (v. 5)—The unbeliever's rebellious nature is awakened when restrictions are placed on him or her.

fruit to death (v. 5)—Sin brings a harvest of eternal judgment in the life of an unbeliever.

Romans 7:1–25 (NKJV)

1 *Or do you not know, brethren (for I speak to those who know the law), that the law has dominion over a man as long as he lives?*

2 *For the woman who has a husband is bound by the law to her husband as long as he lives. But if the husband dies, she is released from the law of her husband.*

3 *So then if, while her husband lives, she marries another man, she will be called an adulteress; but if her husband dies, she is free from that law, so that she is no adulteress, though she has married another man.*

4 *Therefore, my brethren, you also have become dead to the law through the body of Christ, that you may be married to another—to Him who was raised from the dead, that we should bear fruit to God.*

5 *For when we were in the flesh, the sinful passions which were aroused by the law were at work in our members to bear fruit to death.*

6 *But now we have been delivered from the law, having died to what we were held by, so that we should serve in the newness of the Spirit and not in the oldness of the letter.*

7 *What shall we say then? Is the law sin? Certainly not! On the contrary, I would not have known sin except through the law. For I would not have known covetousness unless the law had said, "You shall not covet."*

8 *But sin, taking opportunity by the commandment, produced in me all manner of evil desire. For apart from the law sin was dead.*

9 *I was alive once without the law, but when the commandment came, sin revived and I died.*

10 *And the commandment, which was to bring life, I found to bring death.*

11 *For sin, taking occasion by the commandment, deceived me, and by it killed me.*

12 *Therefore the law is holy, and the commandment holy and just and good.*

13 *Has then what is good become death to me? Certainly not! But sin, that it might appear sin, was producing death in me through what is good, so that sin through the commandment might become exceedingly sinful.*

14 *For we know that the law is spiritual, but I am carnal, sold under sin.*

15 *For what I am doing, I do not understand. For what I will to do, that I do not practice; but what I hate, that I do.*

16 *If, then, I do what I will not to do, I agree with the law that it is good.*

17 *But now, it is no longer I who do it, but sin that dwells in me.*

18 *For I know that in me (that is, in my flesh) nothing good dwells; for to will is present with me, but how to perform what is good I do not find.*

19 *For the good that I will to do, I do not do; but the evil I will not to do, that I practice.*

20 *Now if I do what I will not to do, it is no longer I who do it, but sin that dwells in me.*

21 *I find then a law, that evil is present with me, the one who wills to do good.*

delivered from the law (v. 6)—Because we died in Christ, we are no longer subject to the condemnation and penalties of the law.

oldness of the letter (v. 6)— the external, written law code that produced only condemnation

Is the law sin? (v. 7)—Paul wanted to make sure his readers understood that the law was not imperfect or evil but rather only a beacon to point out evil.

opportunity (v. 8)—a starting point or base of operations

dead (v. 8)—that is, dormant

sin . . . deceived me (v. 11)—by causing people to think they could find life in keeping the law

carnal (v. 14)—Literally, "of flesh"; that is, incarcerated in unredeemed humanness; Paul is not in the flesh, but the flesh is in him.

sin that dwells in me (v. 17)—Paul's sin flowed not from his new, redeemed nature but from his unredeemed humanness or flesh.

law of my mind (v. 23)—equivalent to the new inner self

deliver (v. 24)—to rescue from danger, as in a soldier pulling his wounded comrade from the battlefield

22 *For I delight in the law of God according to the inward man.*
23 *But I see another law in my members, warring against the law of my mind, and bringing me into captivity to the law of sin which is in my members.*
24 *O wretched man that I am! Who will deliver me from this body of death?*
25 *I thank God—through Jesus Christ our Lord! So then, with the mind I myself serve the law of God, but with the flesh the law of sin.*

1) What illustration does Paul use to explain the manner in which believers are dead to the law?

_____

_____

_____

_____

2) Underline every reference to the law in this passage. Circle words and phrases that speak about sin.

3) What does Paul say we will wrestle with the rest of our lives (v. 1)?

_____

_____

_____

_____

4) How do you reconcile Paul's discussion of the believer as an entirely new creation, dead to sin, in chapter 6 with his admission of a huge struggle with sin in chapter 7?

_____

_____

_____

_____

Going Deeper

Note the psalmist's high view of God's law in Psalm 19:7–11.

Psalm 19:7–11

7 *The law of the* Lord *is perfect, converting the soul; The testimony of the* Lord *is sure, making wise the simple;*
8 *The statutes of the* Lord *are right, rejoicing the heart; The commandment of the* Lord *is pure, enlightening the eyes;*
9 *The fear of the* Lord *is clean, enduring forever; The judgments of the* Lord *are true and righteous altogether.*
10 *More to be desired are they than gold, Yea, than much fine gold; Sweeter also than honey and the honeycomb.*
11 *Moreover by them Your servant is warned, And in keeping them there is great reward.*

Exploring the Meaning

5) What are the benefits of knowing and obeying God's Word?

6) Is there a contradiction between Paul's observation that the Law is a demanding, unyielding code of condemnation and David's obvious affection for the Law in Psalm 19? Why or why not?

7) Read 1 Peter 2:11. How does this command echo the internal struggle described by Paul in this passage?

8) Where did Paul ultimately find hope in his struggle to live as God commands?

Truth for Today

Sin is so wretched and powerful that, even in a redeemed person, it hangs on and contaminates his living and frustrates his inner desire to obey the will of God.

Reflecting on the Text

9) In what areas are you frustrated by your sinful inclinations? Based on chapter 7, how effective is legalism in fighting the flesh?

10) What have you learned in this passage that convicts you? Comforts you? Why?

11) Think about one thing in your life you should be doing. Think about one thing in your life that you should not be doing. Write those items in the space below and make them a source of prayer in the week to come.

Personal Response

Write out additional reflections, questions you may have, or a prayer.

Additional Notes

7

In the Spirit

Romans 8:1–39

Drawing Near

Jesus promised the Holy Spirit would come to His followers. When you think about the Holy Spirit, what comes to mind? What questions do you have?

_____

_____

_____

The Context

In the first seven chapters of Romans, God's Holy Spirit is mentioned only once. In chapter 8, Paul mentions the Spirit almost twenty times. It is the Spirit who frees us from sin and death, enables us to fulfill God's law, changes our nature, gives us the ability to overcome the desires of our unredeemed flesh, confirms our adoption as God's children, and guarantees our eternal glory. In short, there can be no success or progress in the Christian life apart from an utter dependence on the third Person of the Trinity.

Paul closes the chapter with profound teaching about the believer's absolute security. Not only are we saved by the blood of Christ and indwelt by the Spirit, but we also are safe in the Father's love. The God who is in control of all things, who has graciously saved us from sin and death and who has begun the process of transformation in us, will never let us go.

Keys to the Text

Holy Spirit: The Holy Spirit is the divine agent who creates, sustains, and preserves spiritual life in those who place their trust in Jesus Christ. The Holy Spirit is not merely an influence or an impersonal power emanating from God. He is a person, the third member of the Trinity, equal in every way to God the Father and God the Son. Among the many characteristics of personhood that the Holy Spirit manifests are: He functions with mind, emotion, and will; He loves the saints, He communicates with them, teaches, guides, comforts, and chastises them; He can be grieved, quenched, lied to, tested, resisted, and blasphemed. He is called God, Lord, the Spirit of God, the Spirit of the Lord, the Spirit of Yahweh (or Jehovah), the Spirit of the Father, the Spirit of the Son, the Spirit of Jesus, and the Comforter and Advocate for believers.

Since Pentecost, the Holy Spirit has indwelt all believers, illuminating their understanding and application of God's Word. He fills them, seals them, communes with them, fellowships with them, intercedes for them, comforts them, admonishes them, sanctifies them, and enables them to resist sin and to serve God.

Unleashing the Text

Read 8:1–39, noting the key words and definitions next to the passage.

therefore (v. 1)—Here Paul summarizes the ramifications of the truths presented in chapters 1–7.

condemnation (v. 1)—a judicial term meaning a guilty verdict; the opposite of justification

the law of the Spirit of life (v. 2)—the gospel, the law of faith

the law of sin and death (v. 2)—God's perfect law that, because of the weakness of the flesh, produces only condemnation.

in the likeness of sinful flesh (v. 3)—Christ was fully man, but without the unredeemed humanness or fleshly nature of sinners.

walk (v. 4)—one's manner of living

set their minds (v. 5)—a basic orientation or disposition of the mind that is set on satisfying the cravings of the flesh

spiritually minded (v. 6)—focused on the things of the Spirit

dwells (v. 9)—makes one's home

Romans 8:1–39 (NKJV)

1 *There is therefore now no condemnation to those who are in Christ Jesus, who do not walk according to the flesh, but according to the Spirit.*
2 *For the law of the Spirit of life in Christ Jesus has made me free from the law of sin and death.*
3 *For what the law could not do in that it was weak through the flesh, God did by sending His own Son in the likeness of sinful flesh, on account of sin: He condemned sin in the flesh,*
4 *that the righteous requirement of the law might be fulfilled in us who do not walk according to the flesh but according to the Spirit.*
5 *For those who live according to the flesh set their minds on the things of the flesh, but those who live according to the Spirit, the things of the Spirit.*
6 *For to be carnally minded is death, but to be spiritually minded is life and peace.*
7 *Because the carnal mind is enmity against God; for it is not subject to the law of God, nor indeed can be.*
8 *So then, those who are in the flesh cannot please God.*
9 *But you are not in the flesh but in the Spirit, if indeed the Spirit of God dwells in you. Now if anyone does not have the Spirit of Christ, he is not His.*
10 *And if Christ is in you, the body is dead because of sin, but the Spirit is life because of righteousness.*

11 *But if the Spirit of Him who raised Jesus from the dead dwells in you, He who raised Christ from the dead will also give life to your mortal bodies through His Spirit who dwells in you.*

12 *Therefore, brethren, we are debtors—not to the flesh, to live according to the flesh.*

13 *For if you live according to the flesh you will die; but if by the Spirit you put to death the deeds of the body, you will live.*

14 *For as many as are led by the Spirit of God, these are sons of God.*

15 *For you did not receive the spirit of bondage again to fear, but you received the Spirit of adoption by whom we cry out, "Abba, Father."*

16 *The Spirit Himself bears witness with our spirit that we are children of God,*

17 *and if children, then heirs—heirs of God and joint heirs with Christ, if indeed we suffer with Him, that we may also be glorified together.*

18 *For I consider that the sufferings of this present time are not worthy to be compared with the glory which shall be revealed in us.*

19 *For the earnest expectation of the creation eagerly waits for the revealing of the sons of God.*

20 *For the creation was subjected to futility, not willingly, but because of Him who subjected it in hope;*

21 *because the creation itself also will be delivered from the bondage of corruption into the glorious liberty of the children of God.*

22 *For we know that the whole creation groans and labors with birth pangs together until now.*

23 *Not only that, but we also who have the firstfruits of the Spirit, even we ourselves groan within ourselves, eagerly waiting for the adoption, the redemption of our body.*

24 *For we were saved in this hope, but hope that is seen is not hope; for why does one still hope for what he sees?*

put to death the deeds of the body (v. 13)—the ongoing, lifelong process of relying on the Spirit's strength to resist fleshly urges and to carry out God's commands

led by the Spirit (v. 14)—usually by illuminating the Scripture so that our sinful, finite minds can grasp God's will

spirit of bondage . . . to fear (v. 15)—The unredeemed have no lasting peace because of the effects of sin and the prospect of punishment.

bears witness with our spirit (v. 16)—by fruitfulness and power, not mystical voices

heirs (v. 17)—We stand to inherit all that God is and has.

futility (v. 20)—a reference to the effects of the curse (Gen. 3:17–19)

creation eagerly waits . . . groans (vv. 19–23)—the universal longing for the removal of the curse

firstfruits of the Spirit (v. 23)—The changes God works in us are evidence of the truth that we will one day be like Christ.

groanings which cannot be uttered (v. 26)—divine articulations within the Trinity; profound appeals for the welfare of God's people

all things work together for good (v. 28)—Our sovereign God orchestrates every event in life to bring glory to Himself and benefit (temporal or eternal) His children.

foreknew (v. 29)—not omniscience, but the divine choice to set His love on us and establish a relationship with us

predestined (v. 30)—literally, "to mark out," "appoint," or "determine beforehand"

If (v. 31)—since

25 *But if we hope for what we do not see, we eagerly*
wait for it with perseverance.
26 *Likewise the Spirit also helps in our weaknesses.*
For we do not know what we should pray for as we
ought, but the Spirit Himself makes intercession for
us with groanings which cannot be uttered.
27 *Now He who searches the hearts knows what the*
mind of the Spirit is, because He makes intercession
for the saints according to the will of God.
28 *And we know that all things work together for good*
to those who love God, to those who are the called
according to His purpose.
29 *For whom He foreknew, He also predestined to be*
conformed to the image of His Son, that He might
be the firstborn among many brethren.
30 *Moreover whom He predestined, these He also*
called; whom He called, these He also justified; and
whom He justified, these He also glorified.
31 *What then shall we say to these things? If God is for*
us, who can be against us?
32 *He who did not spare His own Son, but delivered*
Him up for us all, how shall He not with Him also
freely give us all things?
33 *Who shall bring a charge against God's elect? It is*
God who justifies.
34 *Who is he who condemns? It is Christ who died, and*
furthermore is also risen, who is even at the right
hand of God, who also makes intercession for us.
35 *Who shall separate us from the love of Christ? Shall*
tribulation, or distress, or persecution, or famine, or
nakedness, or peril, or sword?
36 *As it is written: "For Your sake we are killed*
all day long; We are accounted as sheep for the
slaughter."
37 *Yet in all these things we are more than conquerors*
through Him who loved us.
38 *For I am persuaded that neither death nor life, nor*
angels nor principalities nor powers, nor things
present nor things to come,

39 *nor height nor depth, nor any other created thing, shall be able to separate us from the love of God which is in Christ Jesus our Lord.*

1) List the various names for the Spirit that Paul uses.

2) According to this chapter, what acts/ministries does the Holy Spirit perform in us, through us, and for us?

3) How does the Spirit's presence and work change our very nature?

4) What does Paul mean by the references to "groaning" in this chapter (vv. 22–23)?

Going Deeper

Consider Christ's promise of the Spirit to His followers, given in the Upper Room.

John 14:15–17

15 *"If you love Me, keep My commandments.*
16 *And I will pray the Father, and He will give you another Helper, that He may abide with you forever—*
17 *the Spirit of truth, whom the world cannot receive, because it neither sees Him nor knows Him; but you know Him, for He dwells with you and will be in you.*

Exploring the Meaning

5) What more do you learn here about the Spirit?

_____

_____

_____

_____

6) How does the promise in John 14:17 relate to the promise of Romans 8:35–39?

_____

_____

_____

7) Read Galatians 5:22–23. How can the presence of these qualities in your life bring a sense of hope and expectation?

_____

_____

_____

Truth for Today

The Spirit-filled life does not come through mystical or ecstatic experiences, but from studying and submitting oneself to Scripture. As a believer faithfully and submissively saturates his mind and heart with God's truth, his Spirit-controlled behavior will follow as surely as night follows day. When we are filled with God's truth and led by His Spirit, even our involuntary reactions—those that happen when we don't have time to consciously decide what to do or say—will be godly.

Reflecting on the Text

8) According to the statement above, why is it important to read and know God's Word? How is that related to being led by the Spirit?

9) The Holy Spirit was not given so that believers could enjoy ecstatic, feel-good experiences. The Spirit lives in us to change us. The Scottish theologian David Brown stated, "If you don't kill sin, sin will kill you." How, practically speaking, can God's indwelling Spirit empower you for victory over sin today?

10) On a scale of 1–10, with 1 being "carnal" and 10 being "Christlike," how would you evaluate your "life in the Spirit" right now? What needs to change?

11) Meditate on Romans 8:35–39. How does this benediction about God's love encourage you?

Personal Response

Write out additional reflections, questions you may have, or a prayer.

8

Israel and God's Eternal Plan

Romans 9:1–11:36

Drawing Near

In this study we will look at Israel's part in God's plan. Many professed Christians through the centuries have fanned the flames of anti-Semitism, leading to horrendous persecution of the Jewish people. Other Christians have been Israel's biggest supporters. What do you think is the reason for so many conflicting responses over the centuries to the Jewish people?

_____

_____

_____

The Context

Romans 9–11 is one of the most fascinating passages in the New Testament, filled with essential and very practical doctrine and focused on Israel, God's chosen people. Some people have argued that these chapters are a parenthetical body of teaching, largely unrelated to the rest of the epistle. Clearly if Paul had left out chapters 9–11, the overall argument and flow of the letter would be unbroken. His beautiful song of praise, hope, and assurance at the end of chapter 8 flows naturally into chapter 12.

This Jewish apostle to the Gentiles, however, needed to clarify some truths regarding Israel, as well as contradict some prevailing falsehoods that many early Jewish believers accepted as truth. Paul addresses the question of whether, in light of Christ's offer of salvation to all Gentiles, the Jews have been forsaken by God as a people. Did they still have a unique place or purpose in God's plan of redemption? Why, if they were God's chosen people, did they so stubbornly reject His Messiah?

With profound wisdom and holy reason, Paul demonstrates that our sovereign God will be faithful to keep all His promises and that Israel still has a future in the purposes of God.

Keys to the Text

Covenant: A covenant is a legally binding promise, agreement, or contract. Three times in the New Testament the word "covenants" is used in the plural (Gal. 4:24;

Eph. 2:12). All but one of God's covenants with man are eternal and unilateral—that is, to the end of time, and God promised to accomplish something based on His own character and not on the response or actions of the promised beneficiary. The six biblical covenants include: (1) the covenant with Noah (Gen. 9:8–17); (2) the covenant with Abraham (Gen. 12:1–3); (3) the covenant of law given through Moses at Sinai (Exod. 19–31); (4) the priestly covenant (Num. 25:10–13); (5) the covenant of an eternal kingdom through David's greatest Son (2 Sam. 7:8–16); and (6) the new covenant (Jer. 31:31–34; Ezek. 37:26; cf. Heb. 8:6–13). All but the Mosaic Covenant are eternal and unilateral. It is neither, since Israel's sin abrogated it and it has been replaced by the new covenant (cf. Heb. 8:7–13).

God's Sovereignty: A theological term that refers to the unlimited power of God, who has sovereign control over the affairs of nature and history. The Bible declares that God is working out His sovereign plan of redemption for the world and that the conclusion is certain. The story of redemption from Genesis to Revelation is possible only because the sovereign God loves the created world, fallen though it is, and is able to do something about it. Without the sovereign love of the Father ministered to us through the Son and the Holy Spirit, there would be no real human freedom and no hope of everlasting life. God's sovereignty is not the sovereignty of a tyrant, but the loving providence of a gracious God. The believer who doesn't live in the confidence of God's sovereignty will lack God's peace and be left to the chaos of a troubled heart. But our confident trust in the Lord will allow us to thank Him in the midst of trials because we have God's peace on duty to protect our hearts. (*Nelson's New Illustrated Bible Dictionary*)

Unleashing the Text

Read 9:1–11:36, noting the key words and definitions next to the passage.

accursed (v. 3)—The Greek word is *anathema,* meaning "to devote to destruction in eternal hell."

glory (v. 4)—the Shekinah, a cloud signifying God's presence in the Holy of Holies or among His people

covenants (v. 4)—legally binding agreements or contracts, used here of the promises between God and His people

Romans 9:1–11:36 (NKJV)

1 *I tell the truth in Christ, I am not lying, my*
conscience also bearing me witness in the Holy Spirit,
2 *that I have great sorrow and continual grief in my*
heart.
3 *For I could wish that I myself were accursed from*
Christ for my brethren, my countrymen according
to the flesh,
4 *who are Israelites, to whom pertain the adoption,*
the glory, the covenants, the giving of the law, the
service of God, and the promises;

5 *of whom are the fathers and from whom, according to the flesh, Christ came, who is over all, the eternally blessed God. Amen.*
6 *But it is not that the word of God has taken no effect. For they are not all Israel who are of Israel,*
7 *nor are they all children because they are the seed of Abraham; but, "In Isaac your seed shall be called."*
8 *That is, those who are the children of the flesh, these are not the children of God; but the children of the promise are counted as the seed.*
9 *For this is the word of promise: "At this time I will come and Sarah shall have a son."*
10 *And not only this, but when Rebecca also had conceived by one man, even by our father Isaac*
11 *(for the children not yet being born, nor having done any good or evil, that the purpose of God according to election might stand, not of works but of Him who calls),*
12 *it was said to her, "The older shall serve the younger."*
13 *As it is written, "Jacob I have loved, but Esau I have hated."*
14 *What shall we say then? Is there unrighteousness with God? Certainly not!*
15 *For He says to Moses, "I will have mercy on whomever I will have mercy, and I will have compassion on whomever I will have compassion."*
16 *So then it is not of him who wills, nor of him who runs, but of God who shows mercy.*
17 *For the Scripture says to the Pharaoh, "For this very purpose I have raised you up, that I may show My power in you, and that My name may be declared in all the earth."*
18 *Therefore He has mercy on whom He wills, and whom He wills He hardens.*
19 *You will say to me then, "Why does He still find fault? For who has resisted His will?"*
20 *But indeed, O man, who are you to reply against God? Will the thing formed say to him who formed it, "Why have you made me like this?"*

fathers (v. 5)—Israel's patriarchs

children of the flesh (v. 8)—Abraham's children through Hagar and Keturah

not of works, but of Him who calls (v. 11)—God chose Jacob before he was born and apart from any possible human merit to demonstrate that election is the prerogative of God.

who wills (v. 16)—Salvation is not of human initiative.

vessels of wrath (v. 22)—those allowed to incur the just penalty for their sin

Lord of Sabaoth (v. 29)—Lord of hosts or armies, a reference to God's all-encompassing sovereignty

21 *Does not the potter have power over the clay, from the same lump to make one vessel for honor and another for dishonor?*
22 *What if God, wanting to show His wrath and to make His power known, endured with much longsuffering the vessels of wrath prepared for destruction,*
23 *and that He might make known the riches of His glory on the vessels of mercy, which He had prepared beforehand for glory,*
24 *even us whom He called, not of the Jews only, but also of the Gentiles?*
25 *As He says also in Hosea: "I will call them My people, who were not My people, And her beloved, who was not beloved."*
26 *"And it shall come to pass in the place where it was said to them, 'You are not My people,' There they shall be called sons of the living God."*
27 *Isaiah also cries out concerning Israel: "Though the number of the children of Israel be as the sand of the sea, The remnant will be saved.*
28 *For He will finish the work and cut it short in righteousness, Because the Lord will make a short work upon the earth."*
29 *And as Isaiah said before: "Unless the Lord of Sabaoth had left us a seed, We would have become like Sodom, And we would have been made like Gomorrah."*
30 *What shall we say then? That Gentiles, who did not pursue righteousness, have attained to righteousness, even the righteousness of faith;*
31 *but Israel, pursuing the law of righteousness, has not attained to the law of righteousness.*
32 *Why? Because they did not seek it by faith, but as it were, by the works of the law. For they stumbled at that stumbling stone.*
33 *As it is written: "Behold, I lay in Zion a stumbling stone and rock of offense, And whoever believes on Him will not be put to shame."*

10:1 *Brethren, my heart's desire and prayer to God for Israel is that they may be saved.*
2 *For I bear them witness that they have a zeal for God, but not according to knowledge.*
3 *For they being ignorant of God's righteousness, and seeking to establish their own righteousness, have not submitted to the righteousness of God.*
4 *For Christ is the end of the law for righteousness to everyone who believes.*
5 *For Moses writes about the righteousness which is of the law, "The man who does those things shall live by them."*
6 *But the righteousness of faith speaks in this way, "Do not say in your heart, 'Who will ascend into heaven?'" (that is, to bring Christ down from above)*
7 *or, " 'Who will descend into the abyss?' " (that is, to bring Christ up from the dead).*
8 *But what does it say? "The word is near you, in your mouth and in your heart" (that is, the word of faith which we preach):*
9 *that if you confess with your mouth the Lord Jesus and believe in your heart that God has raised Him from the dead, you will be saved.*
10 *For with the heart one believes unto righteousness, and with the mouth confession is made unto salvation.*
11 *For the Scripture says, "Whoever believes on Him will not be put to shame."*
12 *For there is no distinction between Jew and Greek, for the same Lord over all is rich to all who call upon Him.*
13 *For "whoever calls on the name of the Lord shall be saved."*
14 *How then shall they call on Him in whom they have not believed? And how shall they believe in Him of whom they have not heard? And how shall they hear without a preacher?*
15 *And how shall they preach unless they are sent? As it is written: "How beautiful are the feet of those who*

zeal for God (10:2)—fierce attempts to live out God's law; fervent opposition to Judaism's opponents

Christ is the end of the law (v. 4)—That is, trusting in Christ is the end of the futile quest of trying to fulfill the law in hopes of being seen as righteous in the sight of God.

confession (v. 10)—literally, "to say the same thing," thus to agree with God the Father's declaration that Jesus is Savior and Lord

preach the gospel of peace, Who bring glad tidings
of good things!"
16 *But they have not all obeyed the gospel. For Isaiah*
says, "LORD, who has believed our report?"
17 *So then faith comes by hearing, and hearing by the*
word of God.
18 *But I say, have they not heard? Yes indeed: "Their*
sound has gone out to all the earth, And their words
to the ends of the world."
19 *But I say, did Israel not know? First Moses says: "I*
will provoke you to jealousy by those who are not a
nation, I will move you to anger by a foolish nation."
20 *But Isaiah is very bold and says: "I was found by*
those who did not seek Me; I was made manifest to
those who did not ask for Me."
21 *But to Israel he says: "All day long I have stretched*
out My hands To a disobedient and contrary
people."
11:1 *I say then, has God cast away His people? Certainly*
not! For I also am an Israelite, of the seed of
Abraham, of the tribe of Benjamin.
2 *God has not cast away His people whom He*
foreknew. Or do you not know what the Scripture
says of Elijah, how he pleads with God against
Israel, saying,
3 *"LORD, they have killed Your prophets and torn*
down Your altars, and I alone am left, and they seek
my life"?
4 *But what does the divine response say to him? "I*
have reserved for Myself seven thousand men who
have not bowed the knee to Baal."
5 *Even so then, at this present time there is a remnant*
according to the election of grace.
6 *And if by grace, then it is no longer of works;*
otherwise grace is no longer grace. But if it is of
works, it is no longer grace; otherwise work is no
longer work.
7 *What then? Israel has not obtained what it seeks;*
but the elect have obtained it, and the rest were
blinded.

the word of God (v. 17)—more accurately, "the word of Christ"—that is, the message about Christ, the gospel

cast away (11:1)—to thrust away from one's self

remnant (v. 5)—Though the national leadership had spurned Christ, thousands of individual Jews had believed in Him (Acts 2:41 and 4:4).

8 *Just as it is written: "God has given them a spirit of stupor, Eyes that they should not see And ears that they should not hear, To this very day."*
9 *And David says: "Let their table become a snare and a trap, A stumbling block and a recompense to them.*
10 *Let their eyes be darkened, so that they do not see, And bow down their back always."*
11 *I say then, have they stumbled that they should fall? Certainly not! But through their fall, to provoke them to jealousy, salvation has come to the Gentiles.*
12 *Now if their fall is riches for the world, and their failure riches for the Gentiles, how much more their fullness!*
13 *For I speak to you Gentiles; inasmuch as I am an apostle to the Gentiles, I magnify my ministry,*
14 *if by any means I may provoke to jealousy those who are my flesh and save some of them.*
15 *For if their being cast away is the reconciling of the world, what will their acceptance be but life from the dead?*
16 *For if the firstfruit is holy, the lump is also holy; and if the root is holy, so are the branches.*
17 *And if some of the branches were broken off, and you, being a wild olive tree, were grafted in among them, and with them became a partaker of the root and fatness of the olive tree,*
18 *do not boast against the branches. But if you do boast, remember that you do not support the root, but the root supports you.*
19 *You will say then, "Branches were broken off that I might be grafted in."*
20 *Well said. Because of unbelief they were broken off, and you stand by faith. Do not be haughty, but fear.*
21 *For if God did not spare the natural branches, He may not spare you either.*
22 *Therefore consider the goodness and severity of God: on those who fell, severity; but toward you, goodness, if you continue in His goodness. Otherwise you also will be cut off.*

root (v. 16)—the patriarchs Abraham, Isaac, and Jacob

branches (v. 16ff.)—the patriarch's descendants, that is, the nation of Israel

goodness and severity (v. 22)—God's attributes are not at odds.

23 *And they also, if they do not continue in unbelief,*
will be grafted in, for God is able to graft them in
again.
24 *For if you were cut out of the olive tree which is wild*
by nature, and were grafted contrary to nature into
a cultivated olive tree, how much more will these,
who are natural branches, be grafted into their own
olive tree?
25 *For I do not desire, brethren, that you should be*
ignorant of this mystery, lest you should be wise
in your own opinion, that blindness in part has
happened to Israel until the fullness of the Gentiles
has come in.
26 *And so all Israel will be saved, as it is written: "The*
Deliverer will come out of Zion, And He will turn
away ungodliness from Jacob;
27 *For this is My covenant with them, When I take*
away their sins."
28 *Concerning the gospel they are enemies for your*
sake, but concerning the election they are beloved
for the sake of the fathers.
29 *For the gifts and the calling of God are irrevocable.*
30 *For as you were once disobedient to God, yet have*
now obtained mercy through their disobedience,
31 *even so these also have now been disobedient, that*
through the mercy shown you they also may obtain
mercy.
32 *For God has committed them all to disobedience,*
that He might have mercy on all.
33 *Oh, the depth of the riches both of the wisdom*
and knowledge of God! How unsearchable are His
judgments and His ways past finding out!
34 *"For who has known the mind of the Lord? Or who*
has become His counselor?"
35 *"Or who has first given to Him And it shall be*
repaid to him?"
36 *For of Him and through Him and to Him are all*
things, to whom be glory forever. Amen.

the gifts . . . are irrevocable (v. 29)—God's sovereign election of Israel is unconditional and unchangeable.

God has committed them all to disobedience (v. 32)—God is not the author of sin, but He allows sinful inclinations so that He can receive glory in both mercy and judgment.

1) What is Paul's tone in this passage? What is his feeling about his own people?

2) What main characters and events in Israel's history does Paul mention?

3) How does Paul argue in chapter 9 that Israel's unbelief is consistent with God's plan?

4) What agricultural imagery does Paul use in chapter 11 to demonstrate that God's setting aside of Israel is not a permanent condition?

Going Deeper

Notice how this passage in the Old Testament book of Jeremiah foreshadows the theme of chapters 9–11—that God is sovereign and can do as He wishes with His creatures (without violating His goodness or mercy).

Jeremiah 18:1–10 (NKJV)

1 *The word which came to Jeremiah from the* LORD, *saying:*
2 *"Arise and go down to the potter's house, and there I will cause you to hear My words."*
3 *Then I went down to the potter's house, and there he was, making something at the wheel.*
4 *And the vessel that he made of clay was marred in the hand of the potter; so he made it again into another vessel, as it seemed good to the potter to make.*

5 *Then the word of the* LORD *came to me, saying:*
6 *"O house of Israel, can I not do with you as this potter?" says the* LORD.
"Look, as the clay is in the potter's hand, so are you in My hand, O house of Israel!
7 *The instant I speak concerning a nation and concerning a kingdom, to pluck up, to pull down, and to destroy it,*
8 *if that nation against whom I have spoken turns from its evil, I will relent of the disaster that I thought to bring upon it.*
9 *And the instant I speak concerning a nation and concerning a kingdom, to build and to plant it,*
10 *if it does evil in My sight so that it does not obey My voice, then I will relent concerning the good with which I said I would benefit it.*

Exploring the Meaning

5) What does God want Israel to know about Him? Why?

_____

_____

_____

6) How does Jeremiah express the concept of God's sovereignty? Does this help you understand it better? Why?

_____

_____

_____

7) Read Revelation 7:1–12. What does this suggest about the future relationship between Jews and Gentiles?

_____

_____

_____

Truth for Today

God cannot be finished with the nation of Israel—for the obvious reason that all of His promises to her have not yet been fulfilled. If God were through with His chosen nation, His Word would be false and His integrity discredited.

Reflecting on the Text

8) Given what you've seen in these chapters, what should be the modern-day Christian's attitude toward the Jews?

9) Paul's love and concern for his countrymen was such that he wished he could trade places with them, literally that he could go to hell so that they might be saved. How can you develop more compassion for those who do not know the good news of Jesus?

10) Paul ends his reflection on God's faithfulness and mercy with a magnificent doxology. If you were to write a four-sentence tribute of praise to God for including you in His eternal plan of salvation, what would it say?

Personal Response

Write out additional reflections, questions you may have, or a prayer.

Additional Notes

9

Supernatural Living

Romans 12:1–21

Drawing Near

On a scale of 1 to 10 (1= "Virtually nonexistent"; 10= "Almost perfect"), how would you rate your church's "body life"—how people serve and relate to each other in the body of Christ? Why?

_____

_____

_____

What do you wish was different in your church body?

_____

_____

_____

The Context

After pages of rich theological truth, Paul spends the balance of his letter to the Romans explaining how these doctrines should look in a believer's or congregation's daily life. This is a repeated theme in Paul's writings: Theology can *never* be divorced from life; it *always* has practical ramifications and implications.

Paul's description here is nothing short of supernatural living! Paul demonstrates that when believers give themselves fully to God and then, in the power of the Spirit, live out in experience what is true of them theologically in Christ, the result is staggering. Such an other-worldly life will be like a bright neon sign in a dark culture.

Christians who are living sacrifices in the service of God are godly, not worldly; transformed, not conformed; humble, not proud; helpful and generous, not stingy; unified with others, not divided from them; loving, not hypocritical and hateful; other-centered, not self-absorbed; enthusiastic, not blah; forgiving, not vengeful. To find out more about this kind of supernatural life, read on.

Keys to the Text

Spiritual Gifts: A spiritual gift is a graciously given supernaturally designed ability granted to every believer by which the Holy Spirit ministers to the body of Christ. Spiritual gifts are divine enablements for ministry that the Holy Spirit gives in some measure to all believers. They are to be completely under His control and used for the building of the church to Christ's glory. The Greek word (*charisma*) emphasizes the freeness of the gift. A spiritual gift cannot be earned, pursued, or worked up. It is merely "received" through the grace of God. The categories of spiritual gifts are given in Romans 12:3–8 and 1 Corinthians 12:4–10. Each believer has one specific gift, often a combination of the various categories of gifts blended together uniquely for each Christian. Spiritual gifts are not for the exaltation of the one with the gift, but to be used in loving concern for the benefit of others in the church.

Unleashing the Text

Read 12:1–21, noting the key words and definitions next to the passage.

beseech (v. 1)—urge, admonish, encourage; from the same Greek word that means to call alongside for help

therefore (v. 1)—Since all things were created for the glory of God (11:36), we should live our lives for the same purpose.

mercies of God (v. 1)—a phrase summarizing the gracious, extravagant work of God on behalf of sinners that Paul had discussed in chapters 1–11

present your bodies (v. 1)—Believers are called to devote or offer themselves completely and unreservedly to the Lord. This is the only way we can honor God with our unredeemed bodies.

reasonable service (v. 1)—Reasonable means logical; in light of all God has done for us, this is what we should do for Him.

conformed (v. 2)—to assume an external appearance that does not match the internal reality

this world (v. 2)—literally, "this age"; the system of beliefs and values that comprise the spirit

Romans 12:1–21 (NKJV)

1 *I beseech you therefore, brethren, by the mercies of God, that you present your bodies a living sacrifice, holy, acceptable to God, which is your reasonable service.*

2 *And do not be conformed to this world, but be transformed by the renewing of your mind, that you may prove what is that good and acceptable and perfect will of God.*

3 *For I say, through the grace given to me, to everyone who is among you, not to think of himself more highly than he ought to think, but to think soberly, as God has dealt to each one a measure of faith.*

4 *For as we have many members in one body, but all the members do not have the same function,*

5 *so we, being many, are one body in Christ, and individually members of one another.*

6 *Having then gifts differing according to the grace that is given to us, let us use them: if prophecy, let us prophesy in proportion to our faith;*

7 *or ministry, let us use it in our ministering; he who teaches, in teaching;*

8 *he who exhorts, in exhortation; he who gives, with*

liberality; he who leads, with diligence; he who shows mercy, with cheerfulness.

9 *Let love be without hypocrisy. Abhor what is evil. Cling to what is good.*

10 *Be kindly affectionate to one another with brotherly love, in honor giving preference to one another;*

11 *not lagging in diligence, fervent in spirit, serving the Lord;*

12 *rejoicing in hope, patient in tribulation, continuing steadfastly in prayer;*

13 *distributing to the needs of the saints, given to hospitality.*

14 *Bless those who persecute you; bless and do not curse.*

15 *Rejoice with those who rejoice, and weep with those who weep.*

16 *Be of the same mind toward one another. Do not set your mind on high things, but associate with the humble. Do not be wise in your own opinion.*

17 *Repay no one evil for evil. Have regard for good things in the sight of all men.*

18 *If it is possible, as much as depends on you, live peaceably with all men.*

19 *Beloved, do not avenge yourselves, but rather give place to wrath; for it is written, "Vengeance is Mine, I will repay," says the Lord.*

20 *Therefore "If your enemy is hungry, feed him; If he is thirsty, give him a drink; For in so doing you will heap coals of fire on his head."*

21 *Do not be overcome by evil, but overcome evil with good.*

of the times in which we live

transformed (v. 2)—The Greek term is the source of the English term "metamorphosis"; the meaning is to change in appearance (because of the inner changes that have and are taking place).

renewing of your mind (v. 2)—to be made new in the way one thinks by being saturated with the Word of God and controlled by the Spirit of God

soberly (v. 3)—the exercise of sound judgment

measure of faith (v. 3)—the correct proportion of the spiritual gift needed to fulfill one's role in the body of Christ

many members . . . one body (v. 4)—The church is a unified diversity.

prophecy (v. 6)—literally, "speaking forth" the truth of God, not necessarily predicting the future

ministry (v. 7)—service, from the Greek word from which we get our word "deacon"

teaching (v. 7)—the ability to interpret, clarify, systematize, and explain God's truth clearly

liberality (v. 8)—simplicity, single-mindedness, and open-hearted generosity

leads (v. 8)—literally, "standing before"

in honor giving preference (v. 10)—showing genuine appreciation and admiration for fellow believers by putting them first

fervent in spirit (v. 11)—literally, "to boil in spirit"—that is, to have an inner enthusiasm that results in productive labor

given to hospitality (v. 13)—Literally "pursuing the love of strangers"; this kind of openness and generosity should be the hallmark of believers.

Repay no one evil for evil (v. 17)—a ban on individual application of the "eye for an eye" principle of justice

heap coals of fire on his head (v. 20)—a reference to an Egyptian custom of demonstrating shame and contrition by carrying a pan of burning coals on one's head; kindness to hateful, undeserving enemies produces shame

1) Paul begins chapter 12 with a call for believers to give themselves fully and completely—body, mind, and will—to God. According to Paul, what is involved in doing this?

2) What evidence do you find here that the Christian life is not to be lived out in isolation?

3) What has God given each of us to use in service to others?

4) If keeping God's law is impossible (as Paul has already argued in this letter), how can you expect to live out the list of commands Paul gives in verses 9–21?

Going Deeper

Read 1 Peter 4:7–11 for more insight about spiritual gifts.

1 Peter 4:7–11 (NKJV)

7 *But the end of all things is at hand; therefore be serious and watchful in your prayers.*
8 *And above all things have fervent love for one another, for "love will cover a multitude of sins."*
9 *Be hospitable to one another without grumbling.*
10 *As each one has received a gift, minister it to one another, as good stewards of the manifold grace of God.*
11 *If anyone speaks, let him speak as the oracles of God. If anyone ministers, let him do it as with the ability which God supplies, that in all things God may be glorified through Jesus Christ, to whom belong the glory and the dominion forever and ever. Amen.*

Exploring the Meaning

5) What insights does Peter add to the doctrine of spiritual gifts presented in Romans 12? Who has the gifts and what is their purpose?

(Verses to consider: 1 Cor. 12:1–31; Eph. 4:7–16)

6) According to Paul, what attitudes and actions glorify God and build up the body? What attitudes and actions dishonor God and tear down the body of Christ?

7) Why is the metaphor of a human body a good one for the church?

Truth for Today

Supernatural living is conforming our outer lives to our inner lives, living out the redeemed, purified, and holy nature we have in Jesus Christ, becoming in practice what Christ has made us—new creations. Supernatural living is not a mystical, undefined life based on elusive good impulses and sincere intentions. It is practical living that results from conscious obedience to God's standards of righteousness, a life lived within divinely-ordained parameters. It is thinking, speaking, and acting in daily conformity with God's Word and will.

Reflecting on the Text

8) The nineteenth-century Englishman Robert C. Chapman wrote, "Seeing that so many preach Christ and so few live Christ, I will aim to live Him." What principle or truth have you learned from this passage that you want to stop talking about and start living?

9) Based on your experiences and the evaluations of Christian leaders and friends, what do you think your spiritual gifts are? How are you using these God-given abilities to serve the body of Christ?

10) Write out a verse from chapter 12 that you will memorize and meditate upon this week to help you renew your mind.

Personal Response

Write out additional reflections, questions you may have, or a prayer.

Additional Notes

10

Living in the World

Romans 13:1–14

Drawing Near

Do you think it's important to be a good citizen? Why?

_____

_____

_____

Is there ever a time you would not obey the law? Explain.

_____

_____

_____

The Context

The first eleven chapters of this epistle (in particular chapters 1–8) explain in marvelous detail what it means to be saved—justified by God's grace working through faith. This monumental miracle of salvation impacts every relationship of the believer. When we are saved, our initial response should be to fully present our "bodies a living sacrifice, holy, acceptable to God, which is [our] spiritual service of worship." The apostle's next concern is for having right relationships in the church with brothers and sisters in Christ, and even with enemies.

After dealing with these matters, Paul focuses on the need to have right relationships in the world. First, we must demonstrate respect for governing authorities. Second, we must love our neighbors and live holy lives that will stand out against the dark backdrop of a world without God.

Keys to the Text

Taxes: The Greek word referred specifically to taxes paid by individuals, particularly those living in a conquered nation to their foreign rulers—which makes the tax even more onerous. That tax was usually a combined income and property tax. In this context, however, Paul uses the term in the broadest possible sense to speak of all kinds of taxes. Jesus explicitly taught that taxes are to be paid—even to the pagan Roman government (Matt. 22:17–21). He also set an example by willingly paying the temple tax (Matt. 17:24–27).

Cast Off Darkness/Put On the Lord Jesus Christ: This phrase summarizes sanctification, the continuing spiritual process in which those who have been saved by faith are transformed into Christ's image and likeness. The image Paul uses to describe that process is taking off and putting on clothing, which is symbolic of thoughts and behavior. Like one who removes his dirty clothes at day's end, believers must discard the filthy garments of their old, sinful lives, and dress themselves in Christ's righteousness.

Unleashing the Text

Read 13:1–14, noting the key words and definitions next to the passage.

be subject (v. 1)—used elsewhere of a soldier's absolute obedience to his superior officer

no authority except from God (v. 1)—As the Sovereign of the universe, God established the various authority structures (government, family, church, employer).

resists the ordinance of God (v. 2)—To disobey the government is to disregard that which has been ordained of God.

judgment (v. 2)—temporal, at the hands of the human authorities

Do what is good . . . have praise (v. 3)—Law-abiding citizens do not normally need to fear punishment.

God's minister . . . for good (v. 4)—to restrain evil and promote domestic peace

bear the sword (v. 4)—Government has a divine right to execute justice on lawbreakers, even capital punishment.

Render (v. 7)—A Greek word signifying the payment of something owed; not a voluntary contribution, but something due.

customs (v. 7)—tolls or taxes on goods

Romans 13:1–14 (NKJV)

1 *Let every soul be subject to the governing authorities. For there is no authority except from God, and the authorities that exist are appointed by God.*

2 *Therefore whoever resists the authority resists the ordinance of God, and those who resist will bring judgment on themselves.*

3 *For rulers are not a terror to good works, but to evil. Do you want to be unafraid of the authority? Do what is good, and you will have praise from the same.*

4 *For he is God's minister to you for good. But if you do evil, be afraid; for he does not bear the sword in vain; for he is God's minister, an avenger to execute wrath on him who practices evil.*

5 *Therefore you must be subject, not only because of wrath but also for conscience' sake.*

6 *For because of this you also pay taxes, for they are God's ministers attending continually to this very thing.*

7 *Render therefore to all their due: taxes to whom taxes are due, customs to whom customs, fear to whom fear, honor to whom honor.*

8 *Owe no one anything except to love one another, for he who loves another has fulfilled the law.*

9 *For the commandments, "You shall not commit adultery," "You shall not murder," "You shall not*

steal," "You shall not bear false witness," "You shall not covet," and if there is any other commandment, are all summed up in this saying, namely, "You shall love your neighbor as yourself."

10 *Love does no harm to a neighbor; therefore love is the fulfillment of the law.*

11 *And do this, knowing the time, that now it is high time to awake out of sleep; for now our salvation is nearer than when we first believed.*

12 *The night is far spent, the day is at hand. Therefore let us cast off the works of darkness, and let us put on the armor of light.*

13 *Let us walk properly, as in the day, not in revelry and drunkenness, not in lewdness and lust, not in strife and envy.*

14 *But put on the Lord Jesus Christ, and make no provision for the flesh, to fulfill its lusts.*

Owe no one anything (v. 8)—*not* a prohibition against borrowing altogether, but an exhortation to pay debts in a timely fashion

love one another (v. 8)—non-Christians as well as fellow believers

sleep (v. 11)—spiritual lethargy and apathy; non-responsiveness to the things of God

our salvation is nearer (v. 11)—Not the element of justification (a present possession), but the time of our glorification; that is, Christ is coming back.

cast off (v. 12)—an exhortation to repent and get rid of sins

revelry (v. 13)—wild parties, sexual orgies, brawls, riots

make no provision (v. 14)—Do not plan ahead or give forethought to sin.

1) What contrasts does Paul make between Christians and the world?

_____

_____

_____

_____

2) What are the God-ordained consequences of defying government authority?

_____

_____

_____

3) How does Paul use some of the Ten Commandments to demonstrate that love is the fulfillment of the law?

_____

_____

_____

4) What facts does Paul use to motivate the believers in Rome to forsake sin and live righteously? Why are we to submit?

_____

_____

_____

_____

Going Deeper

In the Old Testament the Israelites were taken captive by the Assyrian empire. Three devout Jewish men, Shadrach, Meshach, and Abed-Nego, refused to serve or worship the golden idol the king had set up. Read what happened.

Daniel 3:14–30 (NKJV)

14 *Nebuchadnezzar spoke, saying to them, "Is it true, Shadrach, Meshach, and Abed-Nego, that you do not serve my gods or worship the gold image which I have set up?*

15 *Now if you are ready at the time you hear the sound of the horn, flute, harp, lyre, and psaltery, in symphony with all kinds of music, and you fall down and worship the image which I have made, good! But if you do not worship, you shall be cast immediately into the midst of a burning fiery furnace. And who is the god who will deliver you from my hands?"*

16 *Shadrach, Meshach, and Abed-Nego answered and said to the king, "O Nebuchadnezzar, we have no need to answer you in this matter.*

17 *If that is the case, our God whom we serve is able to deliver us from the burning fiery furnace, and He will deliver us from your hand, O king.*

18 *But if not, let it be known to you, O king, that we do not serve your gods, nor will we worship the gold image which you have set up."*

19 *Then Nebuchadnezzar was full of fury, and the expression on his face changed toward Shadrach, Meshach, and Abed-Nego. He spoke and commanded that they heat the furnace seven times more than it was usually heated.*

20 *And he commanded certain mighty men of valor who were in his army to bind Shadrach, Meshach, and Abed-Nego, and cast them into the burning fiery furnace.*

21 *Then these men were bound in their coats, their trousers, their turbans, and their other garments, and were cast into the midst of the burning fiery furnace.*

22 *Therefore, because the king's command was urgent, and the furnace exceedingly hot, the flame of the fire killed those men who took up Shadrach, Meshach, and Abed-Nego.*

23 *And these three men, Shadrach, Meshach, and Abed-Nego, fell down bound into the midst of the burning fiery furnace.*

24 *Then King Nebuchadnezzar was astonished; and he rose in haste and spoke, saying to his counselors, "Did we not cast three men bound into the midst of the fire?" They answered and said to the king, "True, O king."*

25 *"Look!" he answered, "I see four men loose, walking in the midst of the fire; and they are not hurt, and the form of the fourth is like the Son of God."*

26 *Then Nebuchadnezzar went near the mouth of the burning fiery furnace and spoke, saying, "Shadrach, Meshach, and Abed-Nego, servants of the Most High God, come out, and come here." Then Shadrach, Meshach, and Abed-Nego came from the midst of the fire.*

27 *And the satraps, administrators, governors, and the king's counselors gathered together, and they saw these men on whose bodies the fire had no power; the hair of their head was not singed nor were their garments affected, and the smell of fire was not on them.*

28 *Nebuchadnezzar spoke, saying, "Blessed be the God of Shadrach, Meshach, and Abed-Nego, who sent His Angel and delivered His servants who trusted in Him, and they have frustrated the king's word, and yielded their bodies, that they should not serve nor worship any god except their own God!*

29 *Therefore I make a decree that any people, nation, or language which speaks anything amiss against the God of Shadrach, Meshach, and Abed-Nego shall be cut in pieces, and their houses shall be made an ash heap; because there is no other God who can deliver like this."*

30 *Then the king promoted Shadrach, Meshach, and Abed-Nego in the province of Babylon.*

Exploring the Meaning

5) How did the public stance of the three God-fearing Jews enhance God's reputation?

_____

_____

_____

6) Read Acts 5:28–29. What exception, if any, is there to the divine command to "be subject to the governing authorities" (13:1)?

7) What does it mean to "put on the Lord Jesus Christ" (13:14)?

Truth for Today

Believers are to be model citizens, known as law abiding, not rabble-rousing, obedient rather than rebellious, respectful of government rather than demeaning of it. We must speak against sin, against injustice, against immorality and ungodliness with fearful dedication, but we must do it within the framework of civil law and with respect for civil authorities. We are to be a godly society, doing good and living peaceably within an ungodly society, manifesting our transformed lives so that the saving power of God is seen clearly.

Reflecting on the Text

8) What happens to the message of the gospel and the reputation of God and His people when Christians are belligerent and disrespectful in the public sector?

9) When you consider your current set of elected officials (federal, state, and local), is it easy for you to want to subject yourself to their authority? Do you resent paying taxes to the current administration? Why or why not?

10) What if an official is corrupt, unlikable, or disreputable? What are our options as believers?

11) Write down the names of three government officials for whom you can pray this week. If you wish, write them a note expressing your support and gratitude.

Personal Response

Write out additional reflections, questions you may have, or a prayer.

Additional Notes

11

The Strong and the Weak

Romans 14:1–15:13

Drawing Near

Paul didn't mince words when he discussed the relationships we are to have with fellow-believers. We'll see in this study how to deal with tricky situations. Have you ever been truly offended by another Christian? How did you handle it? What was the result?

_____

_____

_____

The Context

A major theme of the New Testament is that of sin's power to destroy the spiritual and moral character of the church. But outright, blatant sin is not the only danger to a church's spiritual health and unity. Certain attitudes and behavior can destroy fellowship and fruitfulness, and they have crippled the work, the witness, and the unity of countless congregations throughout church history. These problems are caused by differences between Christians over matters that are neither commanded nor forbidden in Scripture. They are matters of personal preference and historic tradition, which, when imposed on others, inevitably cause confusion, strife, ill will, abused consciences, and disharmony.

The diversity of the church displays Christ's power to bring together dissimilar people in genuine unity. Yet Satan often works to create division and threaten that unity. The threat to unity Paul addresses in this passage arises when mature (strong) believers—both Jews and Gentiles—conflict with immature (weak) believers. The strong Jewish believers understood their freedom in Christ and realized the ceremonial requirements of the Mosaic Law were no longer binding. The mature Gentiles understood that idols are not gods and, therefore, that they could eat meat that had been offered to them. But in both cases the weaker brothers' consciences were troubled, and they were even tempted to violate their consciences (a bad thing to train oneself to do), become more legalistic under the feelings of guilt, or even to sin. Knowing that the mature Jews and Gentiles would be able to understand these struggles, Paul addresses most of his comments to them.

This section is extremely helpful to all who find themselves worshiping in a congregation of diverse believers, and who struggle to accept those who are different. And isn't that all of us?

Keys to the Text

Idol Worship and Practices: The Greeks and Romans were polytheistic (worshiping many gods) and polydemonistic (believing in many evil spirits). They believed that evil spirits would try to invade human beings by attaching themselves to food before it was eaten, and that the spirits could be removed only by the food's being sacrificed to a god. The sacrifice was meant not only to gain favor with the god, but also to cleanse the meat from demonic contamination. Such decontaminated meat was offered to the gods as a sacrifice. That which was not burned on the altar was served at wicked pagan feasts. What was left was sold in the market. After conversion, believers resented eating such food bought out of idol markets, because it reminded sensitive Gentile believers of their previous pagan lives and the demonic worship. Paul and mature believers knew better than to be bothered by such food offered once to idols and then sold in the marketplace. They knew the deities didn't exist and that evil spirits did not contaminate the food. Knowledge mingled with love prevents a believer from exercising freedoms that offend weaker believers and, rather, builds the others up in truth and wisdom.

Unleashing the Text

Read 14:1–15:13, noting the key words and definitions next to the passage.

weak in the faith (v. 1)—a reference to believers' inability to let go of the religious ceremonies and rituals of the past

only vegetables (v. 2)—the strict diet of conscience-stricken Jewish and Gentile believers who could not bring themselves to eat meat that had been sacrificed to idols

despise (v. 3)—to have contempt or disdain

judge (v. 3)—to condemn

To his own master he stands or falls. (v. 4)—Christ is the ultimate judge of our motives and actions.

Romans 14:1–15:13 (NKJV)

1 *Receive one who is weak in the faith, but not to disputes over doubtful things.*

2 *For one believes he may eat all things, but he who is weak eats only vegetables.*

3 *Let not him who eats despise him who does not eat, and let not him who does not eat judge him who eats; for God has received him.*

4 *Who are you to judge another's servant? To his own master he stands or falls. Indeed, he will be made to stand, for God is able to make him stand.*

5 *One person esteems one day above another; another esteems every day alike. Let each be fully convinced in his own mind.*

6 *He who observes the day, observes it to the Lord;*
and he who does not observe the day, to the Lord he
does not observe it. He who eats, eats to the Lord,
for he gives God thanks; and he who does not eat, to
the Lord he does not eat, and gives God thanks.
7 *For none of us lives to himself, and no one dies to*
himself.
8 *For if we live, we live to the Lord; and if we die, we*
die to the Lord. Therefore, whether we live or die,
we are the Lord's.
9 *For to this end Christ died and rose and lived again,*
that He might be Lord of both the dead and the
living.
10 *But why do you judge your brother? Or why do you*
show contempt for your brother? For we shall all
stand before the judgment seat of Christ.
11 *For it is written: "As I live, says the* LORD, *Every*
knee shall bow to Me, And every tongue shall
confess to God."
12 *So then each of us shall give account of himself to*
God.
13 *Therefore let us not judge one another anymore, but*
rather resolve this, not to put a stumbling block or a
cause to fall in our brother's way.
14 *I know and am convinced by the Lord Jesus that*
there is nothing unclean of itself; but to him who
considers anything to be unclean, to him it is
unclean.
15 *Yet if your brother is grieved because of your food,*
you are no longer walking in love. Do not destroy
with your food the one for whom Christ died.
16 *Therefore do not let your good be spoken of as evil;*
17 *for the kingdom of God is not eating and drinking,*
but righteousness and peace and joy in the Holy
Spirit.
18 *For he who serves Christ in these things is acceptable*
to God and approved by men.
19 *Therefore let us pursue the things which make*
for peace and the things by which one may edify
another.

Let each be fully convinced (v. 5)—In matters not dictated by Scripture, believers must follow their Spirit-led conscience (regardless of what others say or do).

to the Lord (v. 6)—Whether weak or strong in conscience, our decision must be with a view to bring honor and pleasure to God.

judgment seat of Christ (v. 10)—a future day of accounting before God's throne in which our decisions as believers will be examined

stumbling block (v. 13)—anything a believer does—even biblically permissible things—that causes another to sin

grieved (v. 15)—to cause pain or distress; that is, a weak believer seeing a stronger believer enjoy a freedom that the weak believer is convinced is sin

destroy (v. 15)—in this context, not damnation, but devastation

your good (v. 16)—one's rightful exercise of Christian liberty

eating and drinking (v. 17)—trivial, nonessentials

approved by men (v. 18)—suggests approval after careful examination; here, it suggests that our righteous behavior and love for one another would be seen as genuine by a skeptical world

20 *Do not destroy the work of God for the sake of food.*
All things indeed are pure, but it is evil for the man
who eats with offense.
21 *It is good neither to eat meat nor drink wine nor*
do anything by which your brother stumbles or is
offended or is made weak.
22 *Do you have faith? Have it to yourself before God.*
Happy is he who does not condemn himself in what
he approves.
23 *But he who doubts is condemned if he eats, because*
he does not eat from faith; for whatever is not from
faith is sin.

bear (15:1)—literally, "to pick up and carry a weight"; the strong believer is to not just tolerate the weaker brother, but is to show consideration and love by shouldering their burdens

15:1 *We then who are strong ought to bear with the*
scruples of the weak, and not to please ourselves.
2 *Let each of us please his neighbor for his good,*
leading to edification.

Christ did not please Himself (v. 3)—Christ's goal was always to please the Father.

3 *For even Christ did not please Himself; but as it is*
written, "The reproaches of those who reproached
You fell on Me."

written before (v. 4)—the Old Testament Scriptures

4 *For whatever things were written before were*
written for our learning, that we through the
patience and comfort of the Scriptures might have
hope.
5 *Now may the God of patience and comfort grant*
you to be like-minded toward one another,
according to Christ Jesus,
6 *that you may with one mind and one mouth glorify*
the God and Father of our Lord Jesus Christ.

receive (v. 7)—to warmly accept and embrace, even with differences

7 *Therefore receive one another, just as Christ also*
received us, to the glory of God.

the promises made to the fathers, and . . . the Gentiles (vv. 8–9)—God's plan has always been to bring both Jews and Gentiles into His kingdom.

8 *Now I say that Jesus Christ has become a servant to*
the circumcision for the truth of God, to confirm the
promises made to the fathers,
9 *and that the Gentiles might glorify God for His*
mercy, as it is written: "For this reason I will confess
to You among the Gentiles, And sing to Your name."
10 *And again he says: "Rejoice, O Gentiles, with His*
people!"
11 *And again: "Praise the* LORD, *all you Gentiles! Laud*
Him, all you peoples!"

12 *And again, Isaiah says: "There shall be a root of Jesse; And He who shall rise to reign over the Gentiles, In Him the Gentiles shall hope."*
13 *Now may the God of hope fill you with all joy and peace in believing, that you may abound in hope by the power of the Holy Spirit.*

1) What was the situation in the church at Rome? Why do you think there was so much judging of each other?

2) In areas where the Scripture neither prescribes nor prohibits behavior, what counsel does Paul give for determining a course of action?

3) Behind all the different convictions and behaviors, what does Paul suggest should be our ultimate goals when we confront issues not addressed by the Word of God?

Going Deeper

The Roman church wasn't the only congregation in Paul's time that suffered tension due to differences in the body. Consider the apostle's instruction to the church at Corinth.

1 Corinthians 8:1–9 (NKJV)

1 *Now concerning things offered to idols: We know that we all have knowledge. Knowledge puffs up, but love edifies.*
2 *And if anyone thinks that he knows anything, he knows nothing yet as he ought to know.*
3 *But if anyone loves God, this one is known by Him.*
4 *Therefore concerning the eating of things offered to idols, we know that an idol is nothing in the world, and that there is no other God but one.*
5 *For even if there are so-called gods, whether in heaven or on earth (as there are many gods and many lords),*
6 *yet for us there is one God, the Father, of whom are all things, and we for Him; and one Lord Jesus Christ, through whom are all things, and through whom we live.*
7 *However, there is not in everyone that knowledge; for some, with consciousness of the idol, until now eat it as a thing offered to an idol; and their conscience, being weak, is defiled.*
8 *But food does not commend us to God; for neither if we eat are we the better, nor if we do not eat are we the worse.*
9 *But beware lest somehow this liberty of yours become a stumbling block to those who are weak.*

Exploring the Meaning

4) The struggle in the church at Corinth was over meat that had been sacrificed to idols and then was sold in the nearby marketplace. "Should a Christian eat such meat or not?"—this was the big debate. Some concluded that the meat was fine since idols are manmade and not truly divine. Others could not, in good conscience, enter into this practice. What was Paul's solution?

_____

_____

_____

_____

5) Read Galatians 5:13. We are free in Christ, but for what purpose does Paul say our freedom is to be used?

6) Consider the twelve men Jesus chose to be his closest followers (Mark 3:13–19). We know from the biblical record that these men were from a wide range of backgrounds, political persuasions, and occupations. How does this diverse group serve as a model for the kind of unity that modern-day congregations can enjoy?

Truth for Today

To accept one another, just as Christ also accepted us, is a sure mark of godliness, and failure to do so is just as surely a mark of carnality. Failure to accept one another in love and compassion is an affront to the Savior who accepted us. A congregation that is divisive, quarrelsome, contentious, and judgmental gives the world reason to ridicule Christ's church and to reject the One who is their only hope of salvation.

Reflecting on the Text

7) What biblical command or principle from this passage is most helpful to you as you think about relating to others in your local church?

8) When dealing with differences between people, four things are necessary: *recognizing* the differences; *working to understand* the differences; *learning to appreciate* the differences; and *wisely utilizing* the differences. Which of these steps do you have the most difficulty with and why?

9) What particular behaviors in today's culture are okay or not okay for a Christian to participate in? Ask God to give you wisdom to honor Him and love others in all that you do.

Personal Response

Write out additional reflections, questions you may have, or a prayer.

Additional Notes

12

Ministering Together

Romans 15:14–16:27

Drawing Near

Think back over the truths you studied in Romans. What is one new thing you've learned about God? About yourself?

_____

_____

_____

The Context

After completing the major doctrinal treatise of this letter, Paul now begins what amounts to an epilogue, which comprises comments about his ministry, his plans for future service, personal greetings from himself and others, and a closing benediction.

Because Paul had spoken so forcefully on so many issues to a church he did not found and had never visited, he wants to make sure he does not seem insensitive, presumptuous, or unloving. He commends them corporately for their involvement in the work of the gospel. He shares a bit of information about his own ministry and future plans. He reiterates his heart's desire to minister in Rome and to fellowship with the church there.

We get a rare glimpse into Paul's working relationships and close friendships. He mentions by name more than two dozen colleagues and coworkers. In this extended passage we sense the deep affection that Paul had for those with whom and to whom he ministered. We also get to see the sincere gratitude the apostle felt for those who had been such a help and encouragement to him in life and ministry. As the faces of redeemed and transformed Jews and Gentiles flashed through Paul's mind, he closed his epistle with a hymn of praise: "To God, alone wise, be glory through Jesus Christ forever. Amen."

Keys to the Text

Deacon/Deaconess /Servant: From a word group meaning "to serve." Originally referring to menial tasks such as waiting on tables (Acts 6:1–4), "deacon" came to denote any service in the church. Deacons serve under the leadership of elders, helping them exercise oversight in the practical matters of church life. Scripture defines no official or specific responsibilities for deacons; they are to do whatever the elders assign them or whatever spiritual ministry is necessary. Phoebe was named here as a "servant of the church." In the early church, these women cared for sick believers, the poor, strangers, and those in prison. They also instructed the women and children.

Rome: The capital city of the Roman Empire. It is likely the church at Rome had been founded by a group of Jewish Christians who came there from Judea. It is possible that there had been Christians in Rome for many years, converts from among the "visitors from Rome, both Jews and proselytes" at Pentecost. The apostle Paul's first known connection with Rome was when he met Aquila and Priscilla at Corinth (Acts 18:2). They had left Rome when Claudius expelled all the Jews from the city. Some few years after meeting Aquila and Priscilla, Paul decided that he "must also see Rome." When he wrote this letter to the Christians at Rome, it was obvious how much he longed to meet them. His plan was to visit friends in the city on his way to Spain.

When he finally came to Rome, however, it was at the expense of the Roman government, due to his insistence that he be tried before Caesar concerning the charges brought against him by the Jewish leaders in Jerusalem (Acts 25:2, 11). His ministry in Rome was therefore as a prisoner, and it was during that imprisonment that he wrote the epistle to the Philippians. It was also likely that Paul wrote Ephesians, Colossians, and Philemon from Rome. According to tradition, Paul was martyred during Nero's reign (AD 54–68).

Unleashing the Text

Read 15:14–16:27, noting the key words and definitions next to the passage.

knowledge (v. 14)—deep, intimate knowledge; doctrinal soundness

admonish (v. 14)—encourage, warn, advise; that is, a comprehensive term for counseling

minister (v. 16)—one who serves God in some form of public worship

Romans 15:14–16:27 (NKJV)

14 *Now I myself am confident concerning you, my brethren, that you also are full of goodness, filled with all knowledge, able also to admonish one another.*

15 *Nevertheless, brethren, I have written more boldly to you on some points, as reminding you, because of the grace given to me by God,*

16 *that I might be a minister of Jesus Christ to the Gentiles, ministering the gospel of God, that the offering of the Gentiles might be acceptable, sanctified by the Holy Spirit.*

17 *Therefore I have reason to glory in Christ Jesus in the things which pertain to God.*
18 *For I will not dare to speak of any of those things which Christ has not accomplished through me, in word and deed, to make the Gentiles obedient—*
19 *in mighty signs and wonders, by the power of the Spirit of God, so that from Jerusalem and round about to Illyricum I have fully preached the gospel of Christ.*
20 *And so I have made it my aim to preach the gospel, not where Christ was named, lest I should build on another man's foundation,*
21 *but as it is written: "To whom He was not announced, they shall see; And those who have not heard shall understand."*
22 *For this reason I also have been much hindered from coming to you.*
23 *But now no longer having a place in these parts, and having a great desire these many years to come to you,*
24 *whenever I journey to Spain, I shall come to you. For I hope to see you on my journey, and to be helped on my way there by you, if first I may enjoy your company for a while.*
25 *But now I am going to Jerusalem to minister to the saints.*
26 *For it pleased those from Macedonia and Achaia to make a certain contribution for the poor among the saints who are in Jerusalem.*
27 *It pleased them indeed, and they are their debtors. For if the Gentiles have been partakers of their spiritual things, their duty is also to minister to them in material things.*
28 *Therefore, when I have performed this and have sealed to them this fruit, I shall go by way of you to Spain.*
29 *But I know that when I come to you, I shall come in the fullness of the blessing of the gospel of Christ.*
30 *Now I beg you, brethren, through the Lord Jesus Christ, and through the love of the Spirit, that you strive together with me in prayers to God for me,*

glory (v. 17)—boast; Paul never boasted of his accomplishments, only of what Christ had done through him

signs and wonders (v. 19)—miracles that authenticated true teaching and preaching

another man's foundation (v. 20)—As one with the gift of evangelism, Paul's goal and desire was to minister to those who had never heard.

hindered from coming (v. 22)—an ongoing, providential prevention from getting to Rome

helped on my way (v. 24)—Paul's tactful way of requesting assistance in his proposed evangelistic campaign to Spain

contribution (v. 26)—The Greek word indicates sharing and is usually translated "fellowship" or "communion"; that is, minister and financial supporters are partners.

31 *that I may be delivered from those in Judea who do not believe, and that my service for Jerusalem may be acceptable to the saints,*
32 *that I may come to you with joy by the will of God, and may be refreshed together with you.*
33 *Now the God of peace be with you all. Amen.*
16:1 *I commend to you Phoebe our sister, who is a servant of the church in Cenchrea,*
2 *that you may receive her in the Lord in a manner worthy of the saints, and assist her in whatever business she has need of you; for indeed she has been a helper of many and of myself also.*
3 *Greet Priscilla and Aquila, my fellow workers in Christ Jesus,*
4 *who risked their own necks for my life, to whom not only I give thanks, but also all the churches of the Gentiles.*
5 *Likewise greet the church that is in their house. Greet my beloved Epaenetus, who is the firstfruits of Achaia to Christ.*
6 *Greet Mary, who labored much for us.*
7 *Greet Andronicus and Junia, my countrymen and my fellow prisoners, who are of note among the apostles, who also were in Christ before me.*
8 *Greet Amplias, my beloved in the Lord.*
9 *Greet Urbanus, our fellow worker in Christ, and Stachys, my beloved.*
10 *Greet Apelles, approved in Christ. Greet those who are of the household of Aristobulus.*
11 *Greet Herodion, my countryman. Greet those who are of the household of Narcissus who are in the Lord.*
12 *Greet Tryphena and Tryphosa, who have labored in the Lord. Greet the beloved Persis, who labored much in the Lord.*
13 *Greet Rufus, chosen in the Lord, and his mother and mine.*
14 *Greet Asyncritus, Phlegon, Hermas, Patrobas, Hermes, and the brethren who are with them.*

labored (16:6)—suggests hard work to the point of exhaustion

15 *Greet Philologus and Julia, Nereus and his sister,*
and Olympas, and all the saints who are with them.
16 *Greet one another with a holy kiss. The churches of*
Christ greet you.
17 *Now I urge you, brethren, note those who cause*
divisions and offenses, contrary to the doctrine
which you learned, and avoid them.
18 *For those who are such do not serve our Lord Jesus*
Christ, but their own belly, and by smooth words
and flattering speech deceive the hearts of the
simple.
19 *For your obedience has become known to all.*
Therefore I am glad on your behalf; but I want you
to be wise in what is good, and simple concerning
evil.
20 *And the God of peace will crush Satan under your*
feet shortly. The grace of our Lord Jesus Christ be
with you. Amen.
21 *Timothy, my fellow worker, and Lucius, Jason, and*
Sosipater, my countrymen, greet you.
22 *I, Tertius, who wrote this epistle, greet you in the*
Lord.
23 *Gaius, my host and the host of the whole church,*
greets you. Erastus, the treasurer of the city, greets
you, and Quartus, a brother.
24 *The grace of our Lord Jesus Christ be with you all.*
Amen.
25 *Now to Him who is able to establish you according*
to my gospel and the preaching of Jesus Christ,
according to the revelation of the mystery kept
secret since the world began
26 *but now made manifest, and by the prophetic*
Scriptures made known to all nations, according
to the commandment of the everlasting God, for
obedience to the faith—
27 *to God, alone wise, be glory through Jesus Christ*
forever. Amen.

holy kiss (v. 16)—a show of affection for friends, on the forehead, cheek, or beard; carried over from Jewish tradition

serve . . . their own belly (v. 18)—false teachers driven by self-interest and self-gratification

the whole church (v. 23)—the congregation that met in Gaius' house

establish (v. 25)—to make firm, stable, fast; that is, being rooted in the truth of the gospel

1) What specifically did Paul ask his friends to pray about? What ministry plans and dreams did Paul have as he awaited his release?

2) Underline the numerous verbs and descriptive phrases Paul uses in 15:14–33 to refer to his labor for the Lord.

3) Circle the names Paul mentions in chapter 16. What insights into the work and structure of the first-century church can we glean from Paul's personal greetings?

4) In the middle of this warm benediction, Paul includes a brief, but grave, warning against harmful teachings and practices. What specific instruction does he give?

Going Deeper

Consider Luke's record of Paul's difficult, but much longed for, arrival at Rome in Acts 28:11–16.

Acts 28:11–16 (NKJV)

11 *After three months we sailed in an Alexandrian ship whose figurehead was the Twin Brothers, which had wintered at the island.*
12 *And landing at Syracuse, we stayed three days.*
13 *From there we circled round and reached Rhegium. And after one day the south wind blew; and the next day we came to Puteoli,*

14 *where we found brethren, and were invited to stay with them seven days.*
And so we went toward Rome.
15 *And from there, when the brethren heard about us, they came to meet us*
as far as Appii Forum and Three Inns. When Paul saw them, he thanked
God and took courage.
16 *Now when we came to Rome, the centurion delivered the prisoners to the*
captain of the guard; but Paul was permitted to dwell by himself with the
soldier who guarded him.

Exploring the Meaning

5) How does this passage illustrate the mutual affection between Paul and his brothers and sisters in Christ at Rome?

_____

_____

_____

6) Read 2 Timothy 1:16–18. For what is Onesiphorus remembered?

_____

_____

_____

7) Read 2 Corinthians 8:2–4. What instructions or principles for giving does Paul share with the church at Corinth?

_____

_____

_____

Truth for Today

The people God uses to accomplish His will are His instruments, and no Christian should take personal credit for what God does through him. No brush takes credit for a masterpiece it was used to paint. No violin takes credit for the beautiful music the musician makes with it. Neither should a Christian deny or belittle what God has done through him because that would be to deny and belittle God's own work.

Reflecting on the Text

8) A modern-day Christian says, "Why should I get involved in ministry? That's what we pay the church staff for! And all these appeals for money—I'd like to help, but I've got bills to pay. Besides, the church seems to get by nicely whether I give or not." How do you think the believers listed in Romans 16 would respond?

9) Imagine yourself sitting among the believers at Rome as Paul's letter was being read for the first time. How might the words of this final chapter have affected you and your brothers and sisters? Why?

10) Now that you've completed this study of Romans, skim back over some of the passages. Write a short doxology of your own, expressing your thanks to God for all He has done in your life through Christ.

Personal Response

Write out additional reflections, questions you may have, or a prayer.

Additional Notes

Additional Notes

Additional Notes

Additional Notes

Additional Notes

Additional Notes

Additional Notes

Additional Notes

Additional Notes

Look for these exciting titles by John MacArthur

Experiencing the Passion of Christ

Experiencing the Passion of Christ Student Edition

Twelve Extraordinary Women Workbook

Twelve Ordinary Men Workbook

Welcome to the Family:
What to Expect Now That You're a Christian

What the Bible Says About Parenting:
Biblical Principles for Raising Godly Children

Hard to Believe Workbook:
The High Cost and Infinite Value of Following Jesus

The John MacArthur Study Library for PDA

The MacArthur Bible Commentary

The MacArthur Study Bible, NKJV

The MacArthur Topical Bible, NKJV

The MacArthur Bible Commentary

The MacArthur Bible Handbook

The MacArthur Bible Studies series

Available at your local Christian Bookstore
or visit www.thomasnelson.com

We suggest these other fine titles by John MacArthur

Unleashing God's Truth Book-By-Book

ISBN: 0-7852-4968-0

MacArthur Bible Handbook

The *MacArthur Bible Handbook* is the ultimate book-by-book survey of the Bible, including charts, graphs, and illustrations from today's leading expository teacher.

A unique reference tool that is committed to quality and biblical teaching—will help you easily understand each book of the Bible, its historical context, and its place in Scripture.

The Interactivity and Ease-of-Use of eBible™

MacArthur LifeWorks Library CD-Rom

Discover the truth of God's word through verse-by-verse teachings of the Bible! *The MacArthur LifeWorks Library CD-ROM* includes over 50 books, commentaries, study guides, and daily devotions with the ability to customize searches, word studies, prayer lists, and your own Bible reading plan. With John MacArthur's personal selection from Nelson's Bible Reference Library, what use to take hours of study and research can now be done in minutes!

Compatible with all products with Libronix technology.

ISBN: 0-7852-5018-2

Available at your favorite Christian retailer.

Visit **www.nelsonreference.com** or **www.thomasnelson.com** for other titles by John MacArthur and other fine inspirational authors.